Military Blunders

Military

Blunders

Wartime Fiascoes from the Roman Age Through World War I

Major Steven Eden, U. S. Army

MetroBooks

To Kathleen—for her support and love

MetroBooks

An Imprint of Friedman/Fairfax Publishers

Library of Congress Cataloging-in-Publication Data
Eden, Steven
    Military blunders : wartime fiascoes from the Roman Age through
World War I / Steven Eden.
        p.   cm.
    Includes bibliographical references and index.
    ISBN 1-56799-175-0
    1. Military art and science—History.   2. Errors. I. Title.
U27.E33 1995
355'.009—dc20
                                                        95-3077
                                                        CIP

Editor: Benjamin Boyington
Art Directors: Jeff Batzli and Lynne Yeamans
Designer: Kingsley Parker
Photography Editor: Emilya Naymark
Map Illustrator: Steven Stankiewicz

Pre-press by Ocean Graphic International Company Ltd.
Printed in China by Leefung-Asco Printers Ltd.

For bulk purchases and special sales, please contact:
Friedman/Fairfax Publishers
Attention: Sales Department
15 West 26th Street
New York, NY 10010
212/685-6610   FAX 212/685-1307

Contents

Introduction

Not Just a Wooden Horse

A little more than three thousand years ago, the inhabitants of Troy looked out over the walls of their city one morning to see that the besieging Greek army had left. After more than nine years, their enemies from across the Aegean Sea had finally abandoned the field. The Greek camp was deserted, the long ships were gone, and all that remained was a curious monument: a large wooden statue in the shape of a horse. Inscribed upon the statue was a dedication to Athena, the goddess of war and wisdom, and a prayer for her protection during the long voyage home. As the Trojans examined the horse, a debate sprang up among them. Some citizens urged that the offering be taken inside the city, to Troy's own Temple of Athena. Others sug-gested that the horse was some sort of trick and should be broken open, or at least burned out-side the walls, but most of the Trojans were extremely reluctant to damage in any way an object perhaps sacred to the goddess. The debate raged until a Greek prisoner (left behind just for this purpose) confirmed that his coun-trymen had indeed departed, and Priam, King of Troy, decided to have the horse brought inside the city gates. Priam ordered the walls breached so that the immense statue could be hauled into the city, and the Trojans spent most of the night riotously celebrating the end of the Greek siege.

The rest of the story of the Trojan Horse is well known. During the night, the Greek lieutenant Odysseus, who had conceived this clever plan, and a group of soldiers under his command lowered themselves from inside the horse through a cleverly concealed trapdoor and were guided by the Greek "prisoner" to the city gates. The Greek fleet, meanwhile, having merely anchored out of sight beyond a nearby island, returned under cover of darkness. At a signal from Odysseus, the Greeks landed and stormed through the open gates. Troy's drunken defenders were overwhelmed and the city was brutally sacked.

Though the story of the Trojan Horse is probably only a fanciful myth, it serves as a convenient starting point for a history of military blunders. Through a combination of misjudgment, overconfidence, and foolhardiness, the Trojans committed an easily avoidable mistake and thereby undid nearly a decade of stout resistance. This is a sublime example of the military blunder.

In writing a history such as this, the problem is in choosing which examples best illustrate the causes of famous (or infamous) military mistakes. Warfare, by its very nature, often seems to be calamity followed by disaster, with victory going to the general who makes the fewest errors. Decisions in combat are made by men who are afraid, exhausted, and weighed down with the responsibility of their subordinates' lives. A comprehensive catalog of military blunders, therefore, would be very thick indeed. For this reason, the scope of this book has been limited to battles, campaigns, and incidents in which the blunders were eminently avoidable disasters that owed more to the mistakes of the loser than the brilliance of the victor. Some of the conflicts featured are well known, others undeservedly obscure.

The underlying causes of these calamities are many and varied, but several common threads can be discerned. Commanders who commit blunders often do so because their vision of reality has been blurred. Sometimes, this is due to a deliberate ruse on the part of the enemy. Feigned retreat is a time-honored favorite and was employed by such legendary generals as Philip II—at Chaeronea almost four centuries before Christ was born—and Napoleon Bonaparte—at Austerlitz less than two hundred years ago. At other times, commanders are blinded by hubris. This was the major factor in the defeat of Lee at Gettysburg, Napoleon in Russia, and, though he can hardly be ranked among such stellar company, Custer at Little Big Horn. Generals can also fall victim to panic or despair, emotions that similarly cloud perceptions of reality. At the Battle of Chancellorsville during the American Civil War, Major General Joseph Hooker doomed the Union to two more years of war by allowing his fears to get the better of him, while at Culloden during the eighteenth-century Scottish rebellion against the English, Bonnie Prince Charles gambled desperately with the lives of his men and lost.

Not all blunders are caused by the military equivalent of temporary insanity, of course. Sometimes commanders simply do not understand the business of war well enough. Don Francisco de Melo, leader of the losing forces at Rocroi, France, during the seventeenth century, and Publius Quinctilius Varus, slaughtered along with his legions in the Teutoberg Forest in the first century A.D., were both political generals whose considerable skills as administrators did not bring military success. Others are unable to see that their ideas about war have become outmoded in their own lifetime. Philip V at

Crécy during the Hundred Years' War, Francis I at Pavia, Italy, in the 1500s, and the Khalifa at Omdurman, Africa, in 1898, led their men to destruction because they remained devoted to concepts of warfare that no longer applied—as the nature of war changed, the strategies necessary to victory also had to change. Modern generals were also guilty of failing to adapt, though the blunderers who contributed to the death toll of World War I did so from the safety of châteaus far behind the battle lines where the carnage took place.

Finally, some disasters just seem to have happened almost of their own accord. These calamities are concatenations of small incidents, minor lapses, and outright bad luck—no one man's fault, really. Braddock's defeat along the Monongahela River during the French and Indian War, the massacre of a British column by Zulu warriors at Isandhlwana, Africa, in the late 1800s, and the infamous Charge of the Light Brigade during the Crimean War all fall into this category.

Why are military blunders so intriguing? Because they expose the shortcomings of men operating under extreme pressure. For military historians and strategists, they reveal the inner workings of the battlefield—the eternal triangle of morale, shock, and firepower that decides wars—in ways that triumphs cannot. For the rest of us, they remain morbidly fascinating because they are man-made disasters, resulting in the deaths of hundreds or thousands of brave soldiers, the betrayal of causes, or the toppling of empires, sometimes in a matter of minutes. Most of all, perhaps, we savor them as the quintessential tragedies of history, stark in outline, compact in time, and possessed of a certain dramatic inevitability.

*Above: Lois Bacler d'Albe's oil painting of
Napoleon's camp on the eve of the Battle
of Austerlitz.*

De la premiere bataille des chevaliers

E Premier assault de la bata
lle ne fut pas la ou le Roy
estoit Car auant quil sec

TEUTOBERGER WALD · YELLOW RIVER
HASTINGS · CRÉCY

Ancient & Medieval Warfare

Battles have always been decided largely by the interplay of different arms—the mobility and shock power of cavalry, the ponderous mass of infantry, and the long-range lethality of missile weapons. Wise commanders know that each of these arms possesses strengths that can be exploited and weaknesses that must be compensated for. This rule applied equally well to ancient and medieval warfare as it did to war during any other period. In fact, the wide variety of weaponry, troop types, and armor that pre-gunpowder societies developed in relative isolation from one another produced a complexity on the battlefield unmatched until fairly recent times. Moreover, the nature of the battlefield itself—wooded or open, flat or hilly,

firm or boggy—affected the performance of armies in many subtle and unsubtle ways.

Successful warriors and leaders understood the interaction of arms, tactics, and terrain. They avoided exposing their weaknesses and strove to match their strengths against the enemy's vulnerabilities. Blunderers, however, whether through overconfidence in their military strategies or systems, or negligence in guarding their weak points, unnecessarily placed their soldiers at a disadvantage on the battlefield. These flaws led to the most infamous military disaster of the classical world, in which a criminally incompetent commander led his men to utter destruction beyond the boundaries of civilization.

Opposite: A depiction of medieval knights in battle, from a fifteenth-century French illustrated manuscript.

Teutoberger Wald

Quinctilius Varus, give me back my legions!

—Augustus Caesar

In A.D. 15 an army of solemn Roman legionnaires surveyed the tangled German wilderness where six years earlier the empire had suffered its worst military defeat since the Punic Wars. Nestled against the looming flank of the Kalkrieser Berg to the south, a sandy trail, intersected by numerous streams, wound its way over swampy ground. Deeper marshes lay to the north. The whole countryside was blanketed by forest, thickest on the rocky hillsides and giving way to grassy clearings in the narrow valleys.

The Roman commander, Germanicus Caesar, grimly directed his men to gather up the whitening bones for proper interment. In places they lay in heaps, outlining an entire battalion's last stand; elsewhere, single skeletons marked the lonely end of fugitives futilely seeking to escape the battlefield. All were surrounded by the detritus of battle: broken swords, shattered shields, odd bits of armor or personal gear. The remains of officers and centurions, ritually sacrificed by the victors immediately after the battle, were piled upon makeshift altars. Numerous skulls, nailed high on tree trunks, grinned down at the work parties. Slowly, Germanicus's soldiers collected the bones for burial. Altogether, three legions, along with a horde of camp followers, were laid to rest beneath a large barrow in the Teutoberger Wald (the Teutoberg Forest).

Like most disasters, this one was years in the making. It began in A.D. 6,

In the years prior to this battle, the Romans attempted to push their frontier from the Rhine to the Elbe. Though historians do not agree on the exact location of the battle, an approximate site is shown.

when Publius Quinctilius Varus arrived and assembled his troops along the Rhenish frontier. A former governor of Syria and the husband of the emperor's grandniece, Varus assumed command of the legions deployed in Germania Inferior, who were charged with defending and administering the border while spreading Roman influence as far as the mouth of the Elbe River in the North Sea.

Gaul, on the western side of the frontier posts, had been pacified for some time. The Germans in Imperial

territory seemed to be adjusting to Roman ways, and local markets were flourishing. The tribes remained fractious, but they dissipated their energies squabbling among themselves. The prevailing quiet made it possible for Varus, who was more of a bureaucrat in uniform than a true general, to concentrate on civil matters. In the three years following Varus's arrival, the legions spent a great deal of their time clearing forests, building bridges, and laying roads, rather than training for battle. As a result, the troops lost some of their fighting edge.

Besides neglecting the legions, Varus angered the neighboring Germans, with whom the Roman Empire had an uneasy peace. Exceptionally dense when it came to judging his fellow men, Varus failed to realize that the techniques that he had used successfully in Syria were unsuited for dealing with the proud, irascible Germans. Peremptory demands for tribute and clumsy threats of retribution only firmed the German resolve to oppose the will of Rome.

But the Germans retained a healthy respect for the prowess of the Roman legions. Many had served as auxiliaries with the Roman armies in Dalmatia, Pannonia, and elsewhere—they knew that the legions under Varus's control, dulled by peace or not, could easily handle any attack on the frontier. For this reason, the legions had to be drawn into territory where the Germans could fight on their own terms. Accordingly, a young firebrand named Arminius concocted a ruse to lure Varus and his army onto unfavorable terrain.

The son of a tribal chieftain, Arminius wormed his way into Varus's confidence by offering himself as a valuable source of information and advice in the Roman commander's dealings with local tribes. He accompanied Varus and the XVII, XVIII, and XIX Legions when they occupied a summer camp on the upper Weser River in A.D. 9. The tribes were exceptionally quiescent that season, and this calm, unbeknownst to Varus, had been orchestrated by Arminius.

As winter approached, the Romans prepared to return to more comfortable (and less exposed) winter quarters at

To the German romantics of the nineteenth century, Arminius was an idealized symbol of Teutonic nationalism. Right: An 1890 engraving showing Arminius seeking guidance from a prophetess before engaging the Romans. Below: An earlier engraving of the mythical female figure Germania leading the Germans into battle against Varus's legions.

Above: This nineteenth-century German lithograph, after a painting by Friedrich Gunkel, shows the close nature of the fighting in the Teutoberger Wald.

Aliso on the Lippe River. At this point, reports of a tribal uprising reached Varus, and the Roman commander, undoubtedly prompted by the cunning Arminius, resolved to make a detour from the direct route to Aliso in order to suppress the disorder. Unfortunately, he also decided to take with him his considerable baggage train, the wives and children of his soldiers, and a horde of servants, artisans, and other camp followers. Quinctilius Varus notoriously disliked active campaigning, and bringing his logistical tail (supplies, baggage, and support not used in battle) with him, rather than sending it back separately under escort or keeping it protected at the summer camp, meant a shorter stint in the field. As the contrived peace of summer had given Varus a false sense of security, the risk of encumbering himself seemed small

when the task at hand promised to be no more difficult than burning a few villages to restore order. Numerous similar punitive expeditions had been conducted in the past without incident.

Just before the Romans broke camp, a loyal German named Segestes warned Varus that Arminius planned to lead his legions into a trap, but the Roman commander ignored him, characterizing the accusations as the slanders of a jealous rival. Varus's pedestrian, formulaic mind rejected the possibility of such intricate plotting by a trusted subordinate. Thus, in early autumn, escorted by Arminius and his German auxiliaries, the Romans departed their fortifications on the Weser.

Since few eyewitnesses survived, what exactly occurred over the next few days is uncertain, as is the exact location of the battlefield. However,

Elephants at War

One of the more interesting weapons used in ancient times was the war elephant, employed to terrify and trample the enemy or to serve as a platform for archers. Although these fearsome beasts could be extremely effective, especially against troops unfamiliar with them, they often proved to be both a blessing and a curse. One famous general, Pyrrhus of Epirus, lost a battle because he failed to take into account the elephant's excitable nature.

While campaigning against the Romans in southern Italy in 275 B.C., Pyrrhus deployed elephants across his front and launched them against the Roman lines. At first all went well, but unfortunately one young elephant was placed at the opposite end of the formation from his mother. When the calf suf-fered a slight head wound, it panicked and began to fall back, bleating plaintively. Its mother pricked up her ears, left off squashing Romans, and bulled her way across the battlefield to protect her offspring. In doing so, she rampaged through Pyrrhus's own troops, causing his army to flee.

recent archaeological evidence and the surviving accounts of later Roman historians such as Tacitus, Dio Cassius, and Velleius Paterculus allow for a fairly accurate reconstruction of the sequence of events. Apparently, Arminius guided the Romans deep into the wooded, hilly country west of their summer camp. For the first day or so, the only enemy facing Varus was the terrain and the weather. His sweating engineers were forced to clear felled trees and widen sandy trails for the wagons, while violent rainstorms threatened to turn the sodden ground into a morass.

After determining that he had drawn the Romans sufficiently deep into the wilderness, Arminius announced to Varus that he would take his German mercenaries forward to gather rein-forcements. This move renewed suspicions among some in the headquarters, but Varus blithely assured all concerned of the trustworthiness of his aide. Arminius did, in fact, collect more troops, but these he intended to turn against the Roman column as it toiled forward.

Varus's first intimation of trouble came when reports reached him of the slaughter of several outlying detachments. Shortly thereafter, the rear guard was attacked. By this time, march discipline in the column had practically broken down, and gaps appeared because of the slow progress of the baggage wagons interspersed amid the legions. Units were intermixed or pressed in against one another in some places, making it difficult for commanders to respond to the sudden attacks. Meanwhile, the slippery, broken ground made maintaining cohesive formations almost impossi-ble. The Germans took advantage of the Roman difficulties by conducting hit-and-run raids all along the column. Groups of half-naked attackers streamed through the forest, striking the vulnerable trains or isolated bodies of troops. More often than not, the Germans avoided contact with the legionnaires, preferring instead to fling their deadly *frameae*, or light spears, and then melt into the woods before the armored Romans could catch up with them. Varus could think of no better response than to continue forward to fairly open ground and establish a field camp. There he waited for the rest of the day as the remainder of the column fought its way in.

By nightfall, the Roman forces were reasonably secure. As was their custom, they had built a temporary fort by dig-ging ditches around their camp and using the dirt to build earthen walls. While quartermasters burned all but the most vital stores and wagons (in order to reduce the size of the logistical tail and increase the legions' mobility), the Germans kept up a steady missile fire combined with frequent feints to keep the exhausted legions manning the walls. The situation was desperate, but not hopeless—Roman legions were flexible enough to fight in virtually any terrain, casualties were distressing but not crippling, and the march could be resumed on the morrow without the excess baggage that rendered the column so vulnerable. But firm leadership would be required to compensate for the initial blunder that had thrust the legions into danger in the first place, and firm leadership was something that the plodding political general from Syria could not provide.

As dawn broke, the three legions emerged from their camp in battle order. The German forces, however, were nowhere to be seen; Arminius had temporarily withdrawn. Leaving behind a detachment to guard the wounded and the civilians, the Romans moved again into the forest, trying to reach open country. Almost immediately the Germans returned, harassing the column, cutting out stragglers, and steadily eroding Varus's manpower. Hemmed in by trees and marshes, the Romans could do little except struggle painfully ahead. Sometime toward evening, the column reached the Kalkreiser Berg, which Varus's commanders recognized as tailor-made for an ambush. They advised their general to dig in for the night, but Varus dithered. More than likely he was exhausted and demoralized from the ordeal of the past few days and no longer up to making decisions. His vacillation doomed the legions.

A fierce thunderstorm heralded the final onslaught of Arminius's barbarians.

The wily German had massed his army, swollen with enthusiastic reinforcements as word spread of the Romans' predicament, on the wooded slopes to the south. As the weary legionnaires lifted their short swords and waterlogged shields yet again, a wave of screaming tribesmen descended on them. The terrain, the weather, and the lack of overall direction prevented the Romans from responding effectively to this attack, and the Germans soon chopped the column into several disjointed segments. Vala Numonious, the Roman cavalry commander, panicked and ordered his troops to break out on their own; few escaped. Varus, wounded and in imminent danger of capture, killed himself. The balance of Roman soldiers, bereft of leadership along the sinuous trail, sought high ground or

scratched out pathetic ditches as they had been trained to do. Some isolated groups may have held out through most of the night, but by dawn all resistance had ended. Hoping for mercy, the Romans inhabiting the temporary camp built two days before surrendered to Arminius. The Germans, however, apparently did not believe in mercy; the Roman soldiers and most of the civilians were sacrificed to the German gods, and the rest were enslaved or held for ransom.

Close to 20,000 Roman soldiers and auxiliaries died in the Teutoberger Wald. The three legions were never rebuilt and, more significantly, the Romans never again attempted to absorb Germany into the empire. And all this was the result of that most dangerous combination of military vices—arrogance, obtuseness, and indecisiveness—embodied in one inept commander.

✦ ✦ ✦

Varus's blunder of fighting on inhospitable ground is perhaps the most common in military history. Few battles, however, offer as dramatic an example of this species of error as one that occurred more than a millenium later and half a world away.

Above: The triumphant Arminius tramples the sacred symbol of the Roman legion—the eagle standard. The Germans seized two eagles in the Teutoberger Wald. A third was thrown in the swamp by the Romans to prevent its capture.

Yellow River

If it means my death I will exterminate them!

—Genghis Khan

In the early thirteenth century, Genghis Khan gathered the Mongol host for his final campaign. After spending a lifetime welding the quarrelsome tribes of his homeland into a fighting machine of unparalleled ferocity and using it to carve out an empire stretching from the Black Sea to the Great Wall of China, history's greatest conqueror was feeling his age. Exactly when he was born is unknown, but in 1226, when he set out to destroy the Mongol's oldest and fiercest adversary, the Tangut empire of Hsi Hsia (located in northwestern China), Genghis Khan must have been between sixty and seventy years old.

Hsi Hsia occupied the Kansu corridor between the Gobi desert and Tibet, the easiest route into the heart of China and an avenue the Mongols had long coveted. Throughout the spring and summer of 1226, the Mongol horde swept across Tangut territory, leaving a trail of devastated farmlands littered with corpses. By late autumn they were besieging Ling-chou, a city less than twenty miles (32km) from the Tangut capitol. Li Hsien, the Tangut emperor, dispatched an army to raise the siege and, if possible, drive the Mongols back.

Little is known about the exact composition of the Tangut force. Contemporary chroniclers, always prone to exaggeration, estimated its size to be about 30,000; whether it was this large is debatable, but certainly the Tangut commander, Asha-gambu, enjoyed a considerable numerical supe-

Above: The Tangut Empire controlled the route into the heartland of China. Right: History's greatest conqueror—the Mongol Genghis Khan.

riority over the Mongols. Since the Tangut were a recently urbanized steppe people, it is likely that cavalry formed the main striking force of their army, but they also possessed a large number of infantry, probably of lesser quality.

Asha-gambu led his troops southward through bitterly cold weather, meeting the Mongols along the frozen Yellow River. The battlefield was actually part of the river's floodplain, and the

numerous pools left behind by the retreating waters had frozen over, making the terrain extremely treacherous. The battle opened with a charge by the Mongol *mangudai*, a group of light cavalry whose name means "suicide troops." These light cavalrymen dashed headlong into the center of the Tangut army, then recoiled and fled back from whence they had come. Asha-gambu, gleefully watching the retreat, believed he had an opportunity to smash the Mongol horde by counterattacking immediately with only his cavalry. This act would be a gamble, since only close cooperation between foot soldiers and those mounted on horses could normally defeat the Mongols, but the

The Mongols

The secret to Genghis Khan's success was his ability to transform the nomads of his native Mongolia into a highly disciplined and tightly organized army. While the Mongols employed subject peoples from time to time as infantry or engineers, they themselves invariably fought from horseback, using a combination of mounted archers and heavier lancers to create an almost unbeatable combination of shock and firepower.

The Mongols' success on the battlefield was not entirely unmitigated by failure. They did, from time to time, suffer setbacks, including one notable defeat brought about by their own error in judgment. During an early campaign in northern China, before they had acquired the services of skilled Chinese engineers, the Mongols were faced with the task of taking a strongly fortified city near the Great Wall. Bloodily repulsed in several assaults, yet reluctant to settle down for a long siege, the Mongols hit upon a scheme to force a quick surrender. Channels were cut from a nearby river to divert its flow and drown the recalcitrant Chinese. Unfortunately, when the Mongols broke the last earthen bank to release the waters, they discovered that they had made a slight miscalculation. The river spilled out, not into the city, but through the Mongol camp. The sodden, chagrined Mongols immediately abandoned the siege.

Tangut general was nothing if not rash. Consequently, he unleashed his cavalry in pursuit of the fleeing mangudai.

Asha-gambu and his cavalrymen, intent on their quarry, blundered into an ingenious Mongol trap. The surviving mangudai, controlling their tough Mongol ponies with their knees, shot arrows over their shoulders as they withdrew. Once the pursuing Tanguts were well out onto the icefield, previously concealed ranks of mounted archers suddenly emerged from cover to add to the barrage of arrows. The Tangut horses, shod with iron horseshoes, could not maintain their footing on the ice, and they careened across the slippery surface, with whole ranks going down in heaving, congested masses. The combination of ice and arrows quickly transformed the disciplined Tangut cavalry into a confused mob. Asha-gambu, realizing his mistake, desperately tried to rally his forces and turn them toward the near bank.

Before they could escape, however, Mongol heavy cavalry charged across the ice into both flanks. Before the battle, Genghis Khan had ordered that grit be spread along certain avenues over the river and that his soldiers wrap their horses' hooves with felt. This allowed the Mongols to thunder over the ice unimpeded, and they waded into the floundering enemy with a vengeance.

On the Tangut side of the river, the horrified infantry, too far away to offer support, watched their cavalry die. They had little time as spectators, though, before they were also assailed by a mixture of light horse and heavy cavalry. Asha-gambu's vainglorious lunge across the ice not only had doomed his horsemen, but had left his foot soldiers without protection. Demoralized by the spectacular slaughter they had just witnessed, and unable to either flee from or drive away the relentless Mongol archers, the Tangut infantry was quickly routed. As their cohesion dissolved, they became easy prey for the merciless Mongol lancers. Few of Asha-gambu's men escaped; the survivors faced either death or slavery.

Shortly after the battle at Yellow River, Genghis Khan laid siege to the capitol of Hsi Hsia. In June 1227, the last Tangut emperor surrendered the city. Genghis Khan, near death himself, executed the emperor along with thousands of Tangut officials, scholars, and intellectuals. The destruction of the Tangut culture was so thorough that even now only a fraction of their written records can be translated.

Undoubtedly, the Mongols would ultimately have triumphed over the Tangut without this victory—but just as assuredly that triumph was made far cheaper and easier the moment Asha-gambu ordered his men across the frozen waters of the Yellow River.

◆ ◆ ◆

If Varus and Asha-gambu were able to defend their failures, they might point out that they were both victims of ruses in one form or another, a circumstance that partly explains, though perhaps does not justify, their poor judgment. But not all ruses work on the mind of the commander—some are intended to fool his soldiers.

At the Battle of Hastings in 1066, for example, the English king saw through the simple trick designed by the invading Duke of Normandy to entice his men from their secure position. Unfortunately, no matter how he tried, he could not prevent his men from falling victim to it.

A lifetime on horseback made the Mongols extraordinary riders. They were able to wield their weapons effectively at full gallop.

Hastings

By the Splendor of God, I have taken possession of my kingdom; the earth of England is in my hands.

—William the Conqueror

Above: In order to gain access to the English interior, the invading army of Duke William had to fight its way past King Harold's forces. Opposite: This scale model of the Battle of Hastings, which is housed in the Tower of London, captures the climactic moment of the battle, as Norman cavalry bears down on the disordered Saxon shieldwall.

In the autumn of 1066, Harold Godwinson, King of England, stood between his battle standards, the Dragon of Wessex and the Fighting Man, on the highest point of Senlac Ridge. Along the ridgetop, which barred the narrow exit from the Pevensey peninsula, his army, formed up in six or seven ranks, stretched for a little over a half-mile (about a kilometer). The front ranks consisted of his best troops, housecarls wielding swords, two-handed axes, or *bills*, spears with a wicked, hooked point. Clothed in chain mail and protected by large, kite-shaped shields that formed an impromptu wall, the 3,000 or 4,000 housecarls were formidable fighting men sworn to the king's service. Behind the housecarls were a like number of levies (known as the *fyrd*), wearing makeshift leather armor and armed with a hodgepodge of weapons—including, in some cases, farm implements—and probably wishing they were far away from Senlac Ridge on this fine October morning.

Two hundred yards (182m) below King Harold's troops, strategically arrayed in the meadow that sloped gently up to the ridge, the invading army led by Duke William of Normandy prepared its first assault. A thousand archers formed the first rank, supported by 3,000 or so Breton, Norman, and Flemish infantrymen. Behind these forces rode William's knights, who numbered approximately 4,000.

In order to escape from the peninsula where he had landed after sailing from Normandy two weeks before, William had to break through King Harold's army. At best, failure would result in a miserable winter cooped up around his base at Hastings; more likely, it would derail his whole plan for conquest. William's plan involved softening up the English line with a barrage of arrows, hacking through the shieldwall at one or more points with his infantry, and then exploiting any resultant gaps with his cavalry to disperse Harold's men and thus open a route to the English hinterland. It was a good scheme, but it failed to take into account the grim determination of the housecarls or the protection of the shieldwall.

Because few Norman arrows found their mark among the fierce housecarls crouching behind their shieldwall, the Norman infantry arrived at the top of the ridge to face an unbloodied line of fighters who had annihilated an entire army of Viking raiders just three weeks before in northern England. Failing to affect the shieldwall even a little, and subject to an incessant rain of javelins, stones, and primitive clubs from the fyrd in the rear ranks, the Norman infantry fell back, and this withdrawal quickly degenerated into a rout on William's left. Harold, grandson of a Danish pirate, undoubtedly felt a rush of fierce joy at seeing his enemy's backside, but this joy quickly soured as he watched his own right flank break the shieldwall and chase the fleeing Normans. A canny warrior, Harold knew that his army could not afford to abandon its tight formation in the presence of the Norman cavalry. To do so invited disaster.

Cavalry in the Middle Ages

The Battle of Hastings reflected the growing dominance of cavalry on the European battlefield, a dominance that is directly traceable to the same lack of discipline that caused the defeat of Harold's housecarls. Most medieval warriors were extremely averse to regimentation or any form of subservience not directly related to their feudal status. Tactical drill, regulations, and even the concept of a functional chain of command gradually faded from military consciousness until they became the exception rather than the rule in Europe.

Nevertheless, all else being equal, undisciplined cavalry can beat undisciplined infantry every time, and this simple fact of military life made the mounted knight the unchallenged champion of European battlefields for three centuries. Gradually acquiring a sense of tactical infallibility, combined with his exalted social status, the medieval knight, who was generally attended by a retinue of men-at-arms (professional warriors who were not of the nobility), formed the heart of most European armies in the Middle Ages.

Unfortunately for the English, William did not hesitate to accept the invitation. His central reserve of cavalry drove the pursuing English off to the left, isolated them on a hillock a short distance from the main battle, and proceeded to cut them down in an almost leisurely manner. Though he could ill afford the loss, there was little Harold could do to rescue these isolated warriors, occupied as he was in restoring his right. The English line had to remain long enough to prevent the Normans from slipping around it. This meant that every man lost thinned the line a bit more, especially the hard outer crust of housecarls, making it more susceptible to puncture—and any break in the line would allow the Norman knights to pour through and overrun the entire position. Harold stormed up and down the line, extracting promises from his commanders to hold the men in check.

For the next few hours, all went reasonably well for the English. Repeated Norman charges failed to break the housecarls' shieldwall, and it appeared that the defenders might be able to hold their position on the ridge until the sun went down, perhaps longer. Then, recalling the circumstances surrounding his first assault, William hit upon a possible solution to the stalemate. First, he ordered his archers to fire high into the air, so their missiles would arc over the shieldwall and fall among the unprotected levies to the rear. Second, he directed his infantry to feign retreat in order to lure the English into pursuit and away from the safety of the shieldwall.

*Legend has it that King Harold was felled by an
arrow through his eye. In fact, he was probably
killed in hand-to-hand combat as the sun fell.*

As the afternoon wore on, this gambit worked at least twice. In the excitement of battle, Harold's lieutenants could not prevent their warriors from swallowing the bait that William dangled before them. Each time they rushed after their foes, the English forces were quickly run down by the waiting Norman knights. The English king raged along his front from one crisis point to another, managing to hold the line together, but one man—even the king himself—simply could not supervise the army's entire length. Moreover, the fyrdmen, suffering from the arrow barrage and sensing defeat, were beginning to drift away.

By five o'clock, the English were no longer able to maintain the shieldwall, and William unleashed a general assault that cracked the wall in several places.

Except for isolated knots of loyal housecarls, those Englishmen who were able fled into the gathering dusk. Harold, already wounded by an arrow, died at the hands of Normans so blood-mad that they left his body dismembered and virtually unidentifiable. Before night fell, Harold's proud army was destroyed and the few survivors were reduced to hunted fugitives.

The Norman victory at the Battle of Hastings resulted in Duke William becoming William the Conqueror, King of England. His Norman vassals soon fanned out over the countryside, laying claim to what had been a Saxon domain and redefining forever the nature of the English people. This battle also marked the last successful invasion of the British Isles. If Harold Godwinson therefore bears the ignominy of being the last leader to "lose" England, perhaps it is some consolation that the blunder was not his, but his army's.

◆　◆　◆

The Middle Ages in Europe were marked by the decline of literacy, science, and the arts, including the art of war. Lessons learned by the Romans a thousand years before were forgotten, until only the most rudimentary use of maneuver or combined arms remained possible for the poorly trained and poorly organized armies of the era. Indeed, chivalric ideals often outweighed military efficiency when medieval warriors formulated their battle plans. Military incompetence probably reached its height on a muddy hillside in France where the cream of the European nobility combined bullheaded arrogance, overweening pride, poor judgment of terrain, and tactical ignorance in one of the costliest blunders in Western history.

Above: The best source of information for the Battle of Hastings is a medieval wallhanging known as the Bayeux Tapestry. In this section of the tapestry, mail-clad Norman cavalry charge up Senlac Ridge against Saxon housecarls. Left: Duke William of Normandy, who became known as William the Conqueror after his victory at Hastings.

Crécy

*The English archers...shot their arrows with such
force and quickness, that it seemed as if it snowed.*

—Sir John Froissart, contemporary English historian

*Above: At Crécy, the English occupied a
position with unassailable flanks. Right:
The key to English victory: the well-
trained yeoman archer.*

During the Hundred Years' War, England and France struggled over the French throne, as both Edward III of England and Philip VI of France had more or less legitimate dynastic claims to the crown. An intermittent affair that dragged on from 1337 to 1453, the Hundred Years' War consisted mostly of sieges and raids, only rarely punctuated by standard battles. One of the war's few battles occurred on the rolling plains of Flanders, near the village of Crécy, in 1346.

After plundering its way across Normandy, Edward's army of a little more than 10,000 troops had been brought to bay on August 26 by a much larger French force as he sought to escape to the coast near Boulogne. Seeing that the mounted strength of the French force ran upward of 30,000 knights and men-at-arms, Edward resolved to dismount his men and fight a strictly defensive battle. Edward deployed his force in three groups, or "battles," two in the front line and a third in reserve. Between and on the wings of the battles were 5,500 English longbowmen. The English army occupied the top of a muddy slope, overlooking the Vallée aux Clercs; Crécy and the village of Wadicourt protected the right and left flanks, respectively.

It was late afternoon before the French arrived on the battlefield. King Philip led the vanguard, which was composed of his household troops and approximately 6,000 mercenary Genoese crossbowmen. Behind the vanguard were the various retinues of the French nobility and foreign contingents such as those of blind King John of Bohemia, the Duke of Savoy, and James I of Majorca. Philip at first decided to defer the battle until morning, but the arriving bands continued to push forward, eager for blood and cocksure of their ability to sweep away the English. Lacking the force of personality to control his unruly knights and without the imagination to consider any other option, Philip at last ordered the Genoese forward to soften up the English.

The mercenaries had been thrown into confusion by the undisciplined jostling of the gathering feudal host, and they took some time in aligning their formation as they

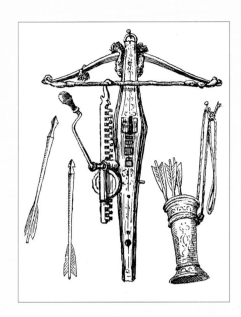

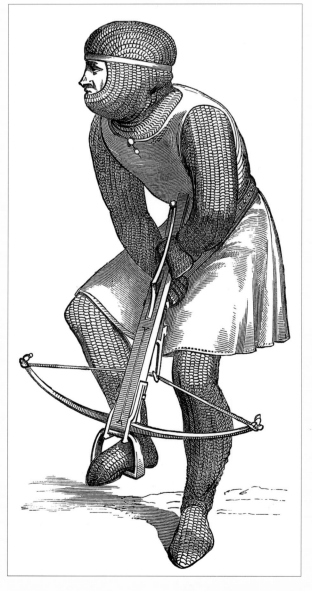

Top: A typical crossbowman of the fourteenth century. Note that the crossbow was fired much like a rifle. Top right: A crossbow used heavier arrows (called "bolts") than the longbow but was accurate to only 60 yards (54.6m), with a maximum range of 300 to 350 yards (273–318.5m). Right: The crossbow was relatively easy to use, especially compared to the longbow, but it took much longer to reload. The firer hooked his foot in a stirrup and cocked the bow by using his body weight to draw the string back. Above: Some heavy crossbows, called arbalests, required a crank to cock. A competent longbowman could loose a dozen arrows in the time it took to reload an arbalest.

Poitiers

After the shattering experience of Crécy, the surviving knights of France pondered the cause of their defeat as they licked their wounds. Not unreasonably, they had no desire for a repeat performance the next time they engaged the English. Could the English victory have been due to the French failure to maneuver intelligently, they wondered? To their lack of wisdom in not attacking the lightly protected archers? To their lack of good sense in breaking off an attack that was obviously suicidal? The French chivalry rejected all those possibilities out of hand. To impute failure to actions motivated by honorable and chivalric impulses would challenge their status as masters of the battlefield. Instead, the common wisdom after Crécy determined that victory had gone to the English because their knights had fought dismounted. What else, after all, could it have been? The French grimly resolved not to allow the English that advantage again.

Therefore, at Poitiers in 1356, the French knights left their horses behind. The English were again drawn up on a hill, with both flanks protected and tangled vineyards limiting access to their front. Numerous longbowmen operated unmolested among the English men-at-arms.

Dismounted this time, the French attacked straight up the middle. Having covered more than a half-mile (about a kilometer) in heavy armor under clouds of arrows, clambering over trellises and grapevines, moving uphill on a slippery field, the Frenchmen were of course exhausted by the time they reached the English line. They were easily repulsed. As they regrouped, King

Edward mounted his own knights, who swept down and around the French, who were too far from their own horses to react. Before the battle was done, 2,000 French knights and their king became prisoners of the English. How they explained their defeat this time is unrecorded.

plodded slowly toward the English lines. This only irritated the impatient French, who were trying to form a rough line of their own behind the Genoese. When they were about 150 yards (136m) from the English, the crossbowmen halted to loose a volley, but most of the shafts fell short. In reply, the longbowmen unleashed a lethal cloud of arrows. Propelled by the deadly longbow and aimed by the finest archers in Europe, the missiles

wreaked havoc among the Genoese, who reeled down the slope.

Watching from below, the Count d'Alencon shouted in disgust at what he perceived as cowardice and treachery on the part of the Genoese mercenaries. Unsheathing his sword, he urged his men forward, and the mounted French knights rode down those hapless Genoese who were unable to get out of the way in time. Spurring up and through the crossbowmen, the French

cavalry contemptuously ignored the vulnerable enemy archers and rode straight for their social equals, the dismounted knights of England. Behind d'Alencon, the remainder of the French forces took his assault to be a signal for action, and the first great charge of the battle commenced.

The French warhorses, however, burdened with their heavily armored riders and slipping on the muddy slope, which the English had seeded with

foot-deep (30cm) potholes, could barely manage a brisk walk. It took the French perhaps two to three minutes to cover the final three hundred yards (273m) before the English positions. Exhausted by the time they reached the enemy, the horses (perhaps displaying better sense than their masters) could not be goaded into hurling themselves against the unbroken ranks of the English. In the meantime, the longbowmen continued to deliver volley after volley into the densely packed mass of French nobility, concentrating on dismounting the French by killing their horses. Arrows fired from the powerful longbow could penetrate armor at close range, and in short order the French lay in heaps before the English line. Well-timed counterattacks dispatched any Frenchman, often pinned beneath a writhing horse, who managed to survive the storm of arrows.

At this point, common sense dictated that the French should break off the attack, turn it against the lightly armed archers, or even use their greater numbers to swing wide and encircle the English. But by this time Philip had lost all control over his army, and the infuriated French could only fling themselves again and again directly at the enemy. As more knights arrived on the field, they joined the press, afraid of missing the anticipated glorious victory. Successive assaults merely churned the ground into a finer goo while adding further obstacles in the form of terrified, riderless horses and piles of armored corpses. The rare threat of a breakthrough was turned back by Edward's judicious use of his reserve, so that the English position was never in any real danger. Even after night fell, waves of French chivalry continued to crest the small rise. All were repulsed, however, and the English longbowmen scrambled down the slope after the retreating knights to retrieve their spent arrows. Astoundingly, there were thirteen to fifteen separate charges before the battle sputtered to a close near midnight.

Displaying far more bravery than intelligence, the French aristocracy, victims of a code of honor that equated tactical acumen or even rudimentary prudence with an unmanly timidity, suffered a blow that day from which it never fully recovered. More than 1,500 nobles lay dead on the battlefield, alongside another 10,000 or so men-at-arms and mercenaries. By comparison, English losses were extremely light, probably less than a hundred.

◆ ◆ ◆

Though historians still dispute the point, evidence indicates that the English employed several primitive cannon at Crécy. These new weapons produced far more flash and thunder than casualties, but their very presence heralded a new element on the battlefield that eventually revolutionized the way armies fought: gunpowder weapons.

For the next century or so, cannon and smaller handheld guns remained too expensive and unreliable to have much influence on the outcome of the battle—they were just as likely to explode and kill those who wielded them as they were to hit their target. Nevertheless, as these weapons were further developed and became more commonly used, they brought an end to the variety of arms and troop types that marked ancient and medieval warfare. Bullets rendered armor useless, no matter how thick it was, and hand-to-hand combat faded in importance as it became easier (and safer) to kill from a distance. The change in warfare was gradual, as armies are inherently conservative institutions, but irreversible.

New weaponry, of course, demanded new tactics and a revised approach to battle. And just as surely, it also opened new fields for the military blunderer.

Opposite, top left: An engraving of Philip VI, from a portrait that hangs in Versailles. Opposite, top right: Engraving of an older Edward III. At the time of the Battle of Crécy, he was in his thirties. Left: R. Caton Woodville's oil painting of the French cavalry at Crécy as it closed with the English.

2

PAVIA • KHANUA • ROCROI
CULLODEN • MONONGAHELA

War in the Age of Gunpowder

Beginning in the sixteenth century, the application of firepower became the supreme weapon in the general's arsenal. While armies of the past had certainly benefited from the use of weapons that were effective beyond the reach of a man's arm—arrows, javelins, spears, even stones—the newer long-distance weaponry—projectiles propelled by gunpowder—possessed far greater killing power. No amount of armor could stop a bullet, and not even the nimblest soldier could dance out of the way of a cannonball at close range. Moreover, training provided no defense against gunfire, as it did against the weapons used in hand-to-hand combat. One could not parry a well-aimed shot.

The only way to avoid the enemy's firepower was through intelligent maneuvers or entrenchments. Successful generals avoided exposing their troops to musketry or barrage unnecessarily. They understood the shattering effect firepower had on closely packed formations, especially on fields devoid of natural cover. They appreciated that human beings, no matter how well motivated, could rarely endure prolonged periods under shot and shell. In other words, while recognizing that personal bravery still played a vital role in war, military commanders grasped the truth that bravery by itself could not vanquish a steady foe armed with gunpowder weapons.

Blundering generals, however, did not understand this new weaponry so well. They either underestimated or overestimated the destructive potential of firepower. Many commanders were unable or unwilling to adjust to the increased lethality of missile fire, and so failed to use their own gunpowder weapons effectively or flung their troops into the teeth of well-armed enemies in the vain hope that spirit alone could win the day. Alternatively, some blunderers relied too heavily on their weaponry, forgetting that certain tactical truths could not be ignored even with the advances in a warriors's ability to kill his fellow man at a distance. In either case, their soldiers and their causes suffered.

Opposite: The new king of battle: the arquebusier. Note the stock used to support his weapon when firing and the powder bags suspended from his crossbelt.

Pavia

To let you know the extent of my misfortune, nothing remains to me but my honour and my life....

—Francis I

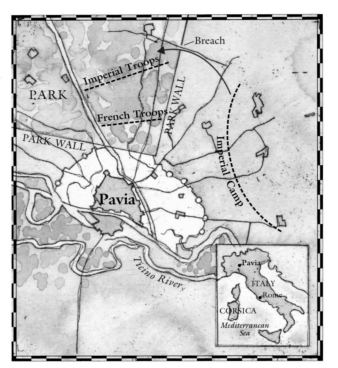

Charles de Lannoy, Viceroy of Naples, representative of the Holy Roman emperor Charles V, and commander of the Imperial Army in Italy, fretted through the cold hours before morning on February 24, 1525. Along with his 23,000 soldiers—a multinational force of Flemish cavalry, 6,500 Italo-Spanish pikemen and arquebusiers, and 12,000 German *landsknechts*—Lannoy waited impatiently while his engineers labored with picks and rams to break down the wall surrounding the Park of Mirabello, thus clearing a path for the Imperial army. An enclosed hunting preserve with an area of about one square mile (2.6 sq km), the park served as a natural defense for the northern flank of the French force besieging the town of Pavia. The work proceeded slowly, hampered by darkness and the need for silence (Lannoy wanted to surprise the French). It was near dawn when the Imperial columns entered the park.

The "French" force opposing Lannoy's efforts to raise the siege of Pavia was actually a mixed bag of mercenaries and feudal levies (at this time, nobles were required to provide a certain number of troops for their king's campaigns—hence, much like a tax might be "levied" in modern times, soldiers were "levied" by the king for temporary service). Commanded by King Francis I of France, the force did include 1,200 *gendarmerie*, elite heavy cavalry drawn from the nobility of the

The Battle of Pavia was the culmination of a long French siege of the Italian town. For some weeks, the relieving Italian army occupied a camp opposite the French entrenchments. Finally, they attacked through the enclosed Park of Mirabello.

realm, and 6,000 French foot soldiers, but the majority were soldiers-for-hire: 5,000 pikemen from Switzerland, 4,500 German infantry, contract gunners for Francis's 53 cannon, and several thousand Italian light cavalry.

Francis was attempting to wrest northern Italy away from Charles V, his fiercest rival for European dominance. The French king had besieged Pavia, an Imperial stronghold along the Ticino River, on October 28, 1524. In late January of 1525, Lannoy's column arrived to relieve the garrison

trapped inside Pavia, which was on its last legs, but the column was not strong enough to break through the French lines. For several weeks, the two armies occupied muddy trenches some 50 yards (45.5m) apart, separated only by a small tributary of the Ticino.

Each army faced a crisis by late February: the Imperial forces had to drive away the French before Pavia was lost, and Francis, short of money, was finding it increasingly difficult to keep his unpaid mercenaries from deserting. Already some 8,000 had left, critically weakening his ability not only to maintain the siege but also to hold off Lannoy. It became imperative for both leaders to resolve the stalemate.

Lannoy moved first. Under cover of darkness, the Imperial army left its entrenchments and moved north, breaking into the park. Lannoy's plan was to have his forces regroup inside the park, then descend on the surprised French and drive them into the river. This move was a calculated risk—it would leave the Imperial troops bottled up in the enclosure and unable to retreat should the fight go against them.

Lax security allowed the breaching operation to proceed without interruption, but sometime during the night French scouts detected the Imperial activity. Francis immediately gathered 40 cannon, his Swiss and German infantry, and his gendarmerie. Daylight found the French deployed in the southern section of the park, ready for

The Development of Gunpowder Weapons

The first weapons using gunpowder were primitive cannon and handguns that were little more than hollow tubes mounted on wooden stocks. Despite this lack of sophistication, by the 1400s artillery became a valuable weapon in siege warfare, rendering most of Europe's castles obsolete in the space of a generation. Because these weapons were highly inaccurate and extremely heavy, they remained of marginal worth on the battlefield. Later advances in metallurgy and carriage design, coupled with the development of primitive aiming devices, produced cannon light enough to move around the battlefield and accurate enough to hit targets more mobile than a stone wall. By the early seventeenth century, a true "field" artillery had emerged, capable of keeping up with the infantry on most terrain and firing solid cannonballs at long range and, for closer fighting, canister or grapeshot, which released a hail of smaller balls, effectively turning the cannon into a giant sawed-off shotgun.

At the same time, handheld guns also became more lethal. Early weapons took a long time to load, leaving the firer vulnerable between volleys; this was true of the arquebus as well as its successor, the matchlock musket. Because of this, armies used pikemen or swordsmen to protect the arquebusiers or musketeers, who were useless in hand-to-hand fighting. As technological advances reduced the reloading time, lightened the weapon, and increased its accuracy, the ratio of gunmen to infantry armed with pikes or edged weapons rose steadily throughout the sixteenth and seventeenth centuries, until, around the time of the Battle of Rocroi, it reached one to one, at least in the larger armies.

Not long after the Spanish defeat at Rocroi, musketeers discovered that mounting a blade—the bayonet—on the end of their weapons made the rifle a passable substitute for the pike. In retrospect, it seems that this development should have been obvious, but several centuries elapsed between the appearance of personal firearms and the adoption of the bayonet. Once the bayonet came into general use, however, the pike all but disappeared from Europe, as the musket-with-bayonet proved to be a highly effective melee weapon. This in turn caused formations to thin into long lines to maximize firepower. Consequently, battles of this period generally devolved into inconclusive shootouts, in which melees normally played a rather insignificant role.

battle, while the Imperialists were still struggling into position. French batteries opened a devastating cannonade, tearing the leading Imperial companies to shreds. Lannoy's gamble seemed to have failed.

Francis I, however, was the product of a bygone era. Reared in the martial traditions of the Middle Ages, he neither understood nor respected the power of gunpowder. Therefore, he failed to take advantage of his overwhelming superiority in artillery. The few Imperial guns available to Lannoy still waited outside the park for their turn to pass the breaches. If Francis had allowed his gunners to fire on the massed ranks of Imperial pikemen and arquebusiers, trapped in such narrow confines, and then followed with a coordinated assault, he might have gained a signal victory. Instead, moved by the spirit that impelled his ancestors at Crécy, Francis placed himself, clad in an exquisitely filigreed suit of plate mail, at the head of his gendarmerie and charged into the Imperial lines. In so doing, he not only left his unsupported infantry behind and deprived his army of leadership at a critical moment, but also put himself and his knights between his own guns and the enemy's

front, forcing the French batteries to fall silent.

The flower of the French nobility quickly overran the Flemish cavalry, which vainly sought to cover the assembling Imperial army. An exultant Francis called out to his followers, "It is now that I wish to be called the Duke of Milan!" The gendarmerie pressed recklessly forward in fine chivalric fashion, seeking to scatter the enemy infantry. But the Spanish foot soldiers responded magnificently to the challenge. More than a thousand arquebusiers discharged their weapons against the onrush. Their leaden missiles easily penetrated the Frenchmen's heavy armor, and the accompanying pikemen held off the milling gendarmerie while the arquebusiers reloaded. Francis, who did not see that it was hopeless to try to break steady infantry armed with arquebuses, threw his horsemen into battle again and again; each time they were

repulsed with heavy losses. Eventually, small parties of Imperial gunmen worked their way around to the flanks and rear of the French cavalry, catching the disorganized gendarmerie in a lethal crossfire.

In a series of uncoordinated attacks, which the Imperialists handily defeated, several of Francis's infantry comman-

ders independently strove to reach their king. Francis himself, surrounded by a handful of loyal retainers, fought on bravely with his gold-hilted sword until his horse was shot out from under him and he was captured. Seeing the elite gendarmerie shattered and their leader captured by the enemy, the French army succumbed unit by unit to the steady advance of the emperor's Spanish and German infantry. Many French formations abandoned the field before engagement, hastened along by a sudden sally from the garrison inside Pavia. By noon, more than 10,000 French soldiers were dead, another 5,000 taken prisoner, and unknown numbers swept away in panic-stricken attempts to swim across the Ticino to safety.

✦ ✦ ✦

Francis's contempt for musketry and his medieval notions of combat were as anachronistic as his plate mail. The opportunity to crush the Imperial army against the walls of the Park of Mirabello disappeared the moment he snapped his visor down and led his knights forward. The destruction of the gendarmerie in the Park of Mirabello also signaled the end of warfare in the medieval style. Neither stout hearts nor thick armor could deflect bullets, and the noble cavalry of Europe—who had controlled the field for three hundred years—was soon relegated to subsidiary combat roles. For the next four centuries, until the advent of the tank, infantry and artillery dominated the battlefield, both in Europe and elsewhere.

Two years after the Italian defeat of the French at Pavia, on the Asian subcontinent, the great Mogul emperor Babur was administering to the warrior caste of India a lesson similar to that learned by Francis and his knights. And like his Neapolitan counterpart, Babur also benefited from the rashness of his foe.

Above: This Belgian tapestry depicts the Imperial Army driving the French from their lines around Pavia and into the Ticino River. Opposite, top: A sixteenth-century portrait of Francis I of France. Opposite, bottom: A typical Italian fortress of the Renaissance period.

Khanua

Many were slain, and fell in the battle, and some giving up their lives for lost, turned to the desert of ruin, and became the food of crows and kites; and hillocks were formed of the slain, and towers raised of their heads.

—Sheik Zain, contemporary historian

Rana Sanga, King of Mewar and leader of the Rajput Confederacy, turned his single eye toward the Mogul camp at Khanua. The Muslim invaders of India, led by their brilliant general, Babur, were busily preparing for battle: digging entrenchments, chaining wagons together along their front to form an impromptu battlement, and erecting wooden palisades for their musketeers. In the center of the Mogul army, great-mouthed cannon gaped ominously, pointing outward. Rana's battered frame testified to his participation in innumerable battles. One empty eye socket, two dozen scars, a badly set leg, and a missing arm gave proof of his willingness to lead men into even the worst fighting. But the grizzled Rajput lord had never faced an enemy armed with gunpowder weapons, though he undoubtedly had secondhand knowledge of the "lightning-darters," the Indian term for cannon.

In the spring of 1527 Rana had raised a great host of Rajput cavalry, which numbered almost 80,000 horsemen and represented India's warrior elite, with which he intended to evict the Moguls from north-central India. Babur, however, had other ideas. After bringing his force of Turks, Mongols, and Afghans southward on what appeared to be a traditional raid, the Mogul leader realized that it would be foolish to abandon the lands he had brought under his control and return

In the early sixteenth century, the Mogul emperor Babur descended from what is today Afghanistan to carve out an empire in northern India.

home. He decided, instead, that he should found an Indian empire. Why rely on periodic forays for plunder, he reasoned, when one could gain as much booty systematically and more easily through taxation? The battle at Khanua would determine who ruled the northern Indian plains.

The Rajput leader, with his horsemen drawn up in glorious battle array, wisely decided to avoid the Mogul center, which was well dug in and bristling with cannon. He decided instead to break one wing of the Mogul army and roll the line up (envelop it) from the flank, thereby negating the Mogul advantage in firepower and position.

The bulk of Rana's army would remain outside effective cannon range, prepared to deliver the coup de grace as the Mogul position unraveled. This seemingly sound plan suffered from two major defects. It did not take advantage of Rana's overwhelming superiority in numbers—estimates of Mogul strength are unreliable, but Babur's army could not have contained more than 20,000 or so quality troops—and it mistakenly assumed that Babur would passively await developments.

Rana Sanga possessed animal cunning, great bravery, and a killer instinct, but he, like Francis I, could not resist taking part in the day's first great charge. The left wing of the Rajputani army thundered forward at about 9:00 A.M. on March 16 or 17 (authorities differ on the exact date), 1527. The highborn Afghan and Turkish troops of Babur's right awaited it, fronted by a line of Turkish musketeers who were using wheeled wooden ramparts for protection. On the far right, sitting patiently astride their steppe ponies, was a strong corps of Mongol cavalrymen, proud descendants of Genghis Khan's feared horde.

Details of the battle are hazy, particularly at the points of contact between the two armies, but this much is clear: Rana Sanga's cavalrymen pressed Babur's right wing hard, but were unable to break or envelop it. Probably frustrated by a combination of musketry, earthworks, mounted

Rejecting Gunpowder

The Hindu horsemen of Rana Sanga were not the only army who chose not to embrace the destructive advantage afforded by gunpowder weapons. The samurai of feudal Japan, for instance, banned outright the use or importation of muskets as a threat to the cultural supremacy of the sword-wielding warrior class. The Mamluks of Egypt, mounted warriors who became the de facto rulers of that region for several centuries, considered the employment of firearms beneath their dignity. Both of these military elites ultimately paid the price for their aversion to modern technology.

Perhaps the oddest case of rejecting gunpowder occurred in Italy in the fifteenth century. There, wars were fought by multinational bands of mercenaries known as *condottieri*. In conflicts in which both sides used these soldiers for hire, the various bands had developed a cozy system of cooperation with their erstwhile "foes" whereby wars were dragged out for as long as the employer's purse lasted. After all, hard fighting and decisive battles brought victory, victory meant peace, and peace led to unemployment for the mercenaries. These mercenaries wore extremely heavy armor to protect themselves during "battles" that were little more than well-orchestrated farces designed to hold down casualties rather than decide campaigns. During one such struggle, at Zagonara in 1423, a daylong battle produced no deaths except for three mercenaries who fell from their horses and smothered in the mud under the weight of

their armor. Firearms, obviously, were too dangerous to use in such wars—they would produce an uneconomical number of casualties, not to mention rendering the expensive suits of armor obsolete—and so the mercenary captains came to something of a gentleman's agreement to avoid their use. This worked fine until 1494, when foreign armies invaded Italy, using modern firearms and artillery to demolish the condottieri in a very unbusinesslike manner.

archery, and Mogul countercharges, Rana led his cavalry repeatedly into the fray, while at least two-thirds of his army stood idle. For his part, Babur, stationed in the center of his army, fed in reinforcements as necessary to support the right and finally dispatched his own household guards to separate the Rajput left wing from its center.

His attack on the Mogul right frustrated, Rana galloped over to his own right and obstinately repeated the process on the left wing of the Mogul army. Once more, the gallant Rajputs nearly penetrated the Mogul lines, but the king of Mewar again neglected to employ the bulk of his force in the assault, allowing Babur to frustrate the Indian charge simply by shifting troops to the threatened sector. Simultaneously, the Mogul commander pushed his artillery and some musketeers forward and began to tear apart the Rajput center.

With both wings beaten and his center weakened, Rana now faced a new threat. Mogul heavy cavalry swung around the Rajput army, lancing into Rana's reserve, which had been pointlessly held back all day—the deployment of a few additional squadrons might have brought him success on either wing. As the Rajputs struggled to avoid complete encirclement, Babur unleashed a final, killing blow.

The Mogul line of wagons had several gaps wide enough to allow about a hundred cavalrymen to ride through abreast. From these portals Babur's own reserve horsemen now issued, carefully avoiding his cannons' line of fire. Already demoralized by prolonged bombardment and the spectacle of Rajput defeats on either wing, Rana's center could not withstand the fury of this final Mogul charge. The collapse of the center, followed closely by a general rout, signaled the close of the action at Khanua and the foundation of the Mogul Empire.

The bravery of Rana Sanga and his Rajput horsemen, nurtured by centuries of tradition among India's warrior caste, was indisputable. The outcome of the battle at Khanua hung in the balance a dozen times, and the Rajputani might have purchased victory at any time with a handful of reinforcements, but Rana had neither the presence of mind nor the inclination to hang back from the fighting long enough to properly employ his considerable numerical superiority. Instead, he led his men forward piecemeal to destruction before the Mogul guns, mesmerized by the slim margin dividing him from triumph.

A little over a hundred years later at Rocroi, France, a Spanish commander made an error similar to that committed by Rana Sanga: he became entranced by the prospect of imminent victory and forgot that even gunpowder had not changed everything.

A depiction of the battle between Mogul and Rajputani forces at Khanua from a Persian illustrated manuscript of the time.

Rocroi

Monsieur de Condé, I dreamt that your son had won a great victory.

—King Louis XIII, to Enghien's father,
three days before Rocroi

L ate in the afternoon of May 18, 1643, the Spanish governor of the Low Countries watched the French army emerge from the woods surrounding the hilltop town of Rocroi, which stood as the last obstacle between the Spanish army's current location and Paris. Don Francisco de Melo, an excellent administrator and diplomat but an inexperienced warrior and leader, commanded the Spanish army, which was on the verge of overwhelming Rocroi's tiny French garrison. As he watched the French array themselves on the open plateau about a mile (1.6km) south of his siege works, he regretted his elementary error of not guarding the narrow, twisting approaches to Rocroi. A few detachments of infantry could have held up the French indefinitely; now he had a battle on his hands.

An abler general might have struck the French as they attempted to disentangle themselves from the thickly overgrown forest, but the hesitant Melo, confused by the French cavalry screen, allowed the opportunity to slip by. The Spaniards restricted themselves to cannonading the French, who were deployed in their line of battle by four o'clock. Nevertheless, even the inherently cautious Don Francisco possessed supreme confidence in his army, a poly-

Above: The two armies at Rocroi were deployed in a virtual mirror image of each other, though the Spanish enjoyed the edge in manpower and number of cannon. Top: Don Francisco de Melo, though an able govenor of the Spanish Netherlands, was out of his depth on the battlefield. Pages 40–41: The Duc d'Enghien surveys the field at Rocroi. The town itself can be seen in the distance.

glot force of 27,000 Burgundians, Germans, Walloons, Italians, and Flemish that was further stiffened by the veteran Spanish *tercios* (special formations consisting of formidable blocks of pikemen and supporting musketeers who were capable of shredding the enemy with shot or delivering stunning blows at close quarters with the pike). The Spanish infantry—their discipline

unrivaled and their tactical expertise unmatched—had reigned supreme on the battlefields of Europe since their victory over the French at Pavia. Melo consoled himself over his earlier mistake with the thought that he now had the opportunity to annihilate the French with the forest at their backs. After that, Rocroi would fall easily, and nothing could bar the road to the French capital.

He did not reckon, however, on the skills of the French commander. Louis II de Bourbon, duc d'Enghien, a remarkable youth of twenty-one recently appointed to lead the 23,000-troop Army of Picardy, possessed abundant energy and great personal bravery, qualities that inspired intense devotion among his troops. His peculiar genius for battle stemmed not so much from meticulous planning or tactical innovation, but from an uncanny ability to sense in a moment the opportunities for victory as they arose during combat. In this, Enghien's first major battle, Melo's blunders would afford the young French noble several chances to display and exploit that talent.

After the inconclusive action on the eighteenth, the armies slept on the battlefield. Both had their cannon posted in front, their cavalry on either wing,

and their infantry backing up the artillery in the center. The French infantry was deployed in three lines, as were Melo's foot soldiers, with the Spaniards holding the center of the first line. The two armies thus arranged presented something of a mirror image, though Melo had the advantage in numbers of infantry and cannon.

Melo planned an attack for about 7:00 A.M. He pulled 1,000 musketeers from his third line and concealed them in the woods just off the French right flank; from here they could open fire on the French cavalry should that force attempt to move forward. Learning all this from a Spanish deserter, Enghien set about thwarting the Spanish scheme. Under cover of darkness, he routed the musketeers from their hiding place, then led a predawn cavalry charge against the Flemish horsemen guarding Melo's left. By daybreak, French *cuirassiers* (heavy cavalry so-called because of their distinctive breastplates, or *cuirasses*) were routing the broken Flemish from the field.

In other parts of the field, however, things did not go as well for Enghien. The Alsatian squadrons of Ernst von Isembourg were driving back the cavalry on Enghien's left flank, and the Spanish tercios were steadily grinding away at his outnumbered center. The French cannon were soon overrun, and the first two lines of infantry gradually gave way. Through the herculean efforts of the third French line under the Baron de Sirot, the Spaniards were checked, but this provided only a temporary respite. Melo appeared to have victory in his grasp.

Unfortunately for the Spanish army, Don Fran-

cisco gave no thought to Enghien's cuirassiers, who were hovering somewhere off his left rear flank. Like many inexperienced commanders, he suffered from tunnel vision—his attention was fixed on the crumbling French center. Stationed in the front line among his tercios, he either forgot or dismissed the need to commit part of his own reserves, so far unengaged, to protect his vulnerable left and rear. As a result, Enghien, having returned from chasing off the Flemish cavalry, smashed unopposed into the third line of Melo's infantry. Taken from behind, and lack-

ing any musketeers for protection, the surprised German pikemen reeled into the second line, throwing it into disorder as well. Within a short time, the mass of Melo's foot strength was streaming away from the battlefield. Enghien now swung all the way around the opposing army, cutting through Isembourg's cavalry, scattering Melo's Italian regiments, and inspiring the hard-pressed French center to redouble its efforts.

Only a few hours after seemingly being on the verge of success, the Spanish "invincibles" found themselves surrounded and their compatriots in headlong retreat, a situation that was largely the result of the negligence of their commander. Unpanicked, the proud tercios prepared to receive the inevitable French assault. Three times the French cavalry and infantry attempted to close, but each time the forces were driven back by murderous volleys. At this point the Spaniards' ammunition began to run low, and several officers signaled for a parley. As Enghien rode up to negotiate, a single shot rang out, followed by a ragged fusillade. The young duke was unhurt, but his men, incensed by the apparent treachery, surged forward unbidden to protect their beloved commander. Despite Enghien's entreaties in favor of mercy for the Spanish, the French soldiers offered no quarter, and the Spanish veterans were soon overwhelmed.

Melo himself escaped with a remnant of some 7,000 men and all of his cannon, but nearly 20,000 of his soldiers, including the heart and soul of his army, the Spanish tercios, were dead, wounded, or missing. The immediate threat to Paris

The Secret of His Success

While France and Spain fought for supremacy on the Continent, a civil war raged across the Channel in England. Parliament sought to assert its primacy in English affairs against a Royalist faction that supported the absolutist claims of King Charles I. The king's ablest general was a dashing cavalryman, Prince Rupert of the Rhine. Time and again he confounded the Parliamentary armies, until finally the legend arose that the source of his amazing success against all odds was his white dog, Boy. Rupert and his pet were inseparable—Boy followed his master into every battle, no matter how thick the fighting. It is not surprising, therefore, that the dog came to be considered a sort of talisman, a charm against Rupert's being slain or even wounded in battle.

Given the importance of Boy as a symbol of Royalist military prowess, Rupert probably should have taken some measures to protect him; but he did not. Eventually, the inevitable came to pass. At a battle at Marston Moor in 1644, Boy joyfully bounced alongside his master as Rupert led his men into action. In the dust and swirl of the melee, the two became separated, and Boy was trampled to death beneath Parliamentary hooves. Marston Moor proved to be the first battle Rupert lost. And, though only the extremely superstitious would point to the death of Boy as the cause, Rupert never won another.

evaporated; moreover, the Spanish warriors never fully recovered from the moral shock of this defeat—their dominance on the battlefield had been based partly on the myth of their invincibility, and this myth was shattered not by the failings of the Spanish soldier, or even the brilliance of Enghien, but by the incompetence of Don Francisco.

✦ ✦ ✦

As the Spanish era faded along with the use of the pike, the other great powers of Europe sought the proper formula for success on the battlefield. It turned out that the key was the use of small armies of professionals, usually serving long-term enlistments. Professional armies were a must, because only through constant drill could an infantryman acquire the requisite skill in rapid firing and complex maneuvering to properly maximize his firepower. Expertise in loading, presenting the weapon, firing on command, and

reloading while standing shoulder to shoulder with other tired, frightened men amid the roar of battle, with musket balls whizzing past one's head, required a great deal of practice. Since this expertise required years of drill to develop, armies remained small because of the enormous expense of maintaining them at full strength even during peacetime.

By 1700, virtually every large state (and most of the smaller ones) in Europe had come to rely on such armies; their strength stemmed from well-trained infantrymen, organized to fight in line formation, eschewing hand-to-hand combat, and able to deliver devastating volleys at fairly close range. In some parts of the Continent, however, groups that had not been fully integrated into the "modern" way of war still existed. Raiders, smugglers, bandits, and other masters of irregular warfare survived in the mountains of Hungary and Spain, along the borders

of the failing Ottoman Empire, across the steppes of southern Russia, and elsewhere; when properly employed, these unconventional troops could be useful adjuncts to regular armies. Untutored in the use of gunpowder weapons, they relied on ambush, trickery, and knowledge of local conditions to defeat the enemy. In difficult terrain they could more than hold their own against the best-trained soldiers of Europe. When called upon to fight in the conventional manner, however, more often than not they suffered resounding defeats. This was certainly the case for one of the last tribes of Europe, the Highland Scots.

Opposite, top: French infantry stand to on the morning of the battle. Note the mix of pikemen and musketeers. Opposite, bottom: D'Enghien's soldiers present to him captured standards and enemy officers in the aftermath of his victory at Rocroi.

Culloden

Here they are coming, my lads, we'll soon be with them. Go on my lads, the day will be ours and we'll want for nothing after.

—Bonnie Prince Charles

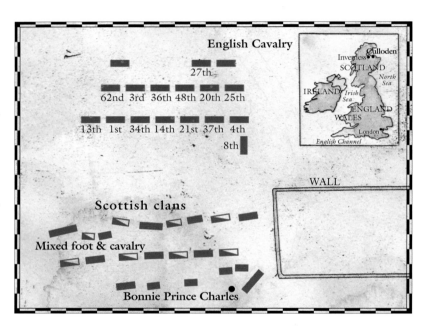

The swampy ground at Culloden funneled the attack of the Scottish clans against the English left.

In 1745 Prince Charles Edward Stuart landed in Scotland to claim his birthright, the crowns of Scotland and England. His grandfather, James II, had been driven from the twin thrones during England's Glorious Revolution of 1688. The Stuart dynasty, living for the most part in exile thereafter, had been a thorn in the English side ever since, claiming to be the rightful rulers of Great Britain and sporadically inciting rebellion throughout the United Kingdom and Ireland. France, seeing the Stuarts as a useful diplomatic cat's-paw, supported the royal pretenders for the better part of a century.

Bonnie Prince Charles, as the handsome and vigorous Stuart claimant was known, began his quest inauspiciously. When he landed in western Scotland in July, his reception proved lukewarm. Some of the Highland clans rallied to the "Young Pretender," but Charles could only scrape together about 1,500 ill-trained troops. Nevertheless, this tiny army managed to occupy Edinburgh, defeat a sizable British force at Prestonpans, and reduce England's presence in Scotland to a few isolated garrisons. These successes won over many who had been undecided as to where they stood in this conflict, and by October Charles's army included 5,000 infantry, perhaps 500 cavalry, and several pieces of artillery, thought-

fully provided, along with trained crews, by the French. The army also acquired the services of a talented general, Lord George Murray. Buoyed by his triumphs, Charles led the army into England, expecting to rally further support for his cause and hoping the French would land troops in the wake of his advance.

Neither of these expectations were fulfilled. Though Charles pushed as far south as Derby, only a few hundred Englishmen, most of them unemployed freebooters (soldiers of fortune, highwaymen, and vagabonds who became mercenaries when money was offered to those who would join the rebellion) joined his cause. The hoped-for French forces also failed to materialize, and on December 5, Charles's officers persuad-

ed him to retreat northward. This was the first of his blunders—the whole rising was a desperate gamble, and any hope of success lay in occupying London. Abandoning the effort to take England's capital doomed the rebellion to failure.

As the unhappy army trudged northward, the English gathered their strength under the corpulent Duke of Cumberland. Close to 30,000 reinforcements poured into northern England, but it was the 9,000 soldiers commanded by the duke who nipped closest at Charles's heels. Murray turned upon the English twice, thrashing them at Clifton and Falkirk, but the implacable Cumberland kept up the pressure, continuing to drive the Scots northward through the winter, until by early April they fetched up against the Highland capitol at Inverness.

By now, Charles could barely hold the bumptious Highlanders and their miserable Lowland allies together. Weariness from the long retreat sapped morale, while the quartermaster's larders were empty—sickness and starvation threatened the army as much as the English. Most of the artillery and gunpowder was gone. Realizing that only a resounding victory could salvage the Young Pretender's cause, the Scots, now deep in the Highlands, turned on their pursuers.

Murray, painfully aware that his exhausted troops had no hope of besting Cumberland's forces in a stand-up fight, tried to bring off a night attack against the British. Unfortunately, however, the approach march was badly bungled, and Murray, unwilling to expose the few men he had on hand to British firepower, canceled the operation as dawn broke. Prince Charles's first intimation of the change in plans came when he intercepted the vanguard of the column returning to camp at Culloden. By nature uncomfortable with Murray's cautious military conservatism, the Young Pretender interpreted the aborted attack as evidence of incompetence, cowardice, and possibly even treachery.

The upshot of the whole affair was that the Scottish army suffered through a sleepless night, Charles lost faith in his ablest general, and the mercurial prince swore he would give battle at the earliest opportunity.

He did not have long to wait. When Cumberland became aware of the failed night attack, he roused his army early and hastened toward Culloden, determined to allow the Scots no respite. Just as Charles lay down, still wearing his boots, to snatch a few hours sleep, scouts reported sighting English cavalry only 4 miles (6.4km) from the Scottish camp.

Many of Charles's officers pressed for withdrawal into the hill country, but Charles stub-bornly refused to yield in his determination to fight. Although he was undoubtedly correct in seeking battle, Charles blundered badly in his choice of battlefield. His army's one strength lay in close combat; Murray understood this, and fought only when terrain or poor visibility allowed the clansmen to avoid English firepower and engage their traditional enemies in hand-to-hand combat. The field of Culloden, however, was open, gently rolling grassland. Moreover, many parts of it were boggy, a fact unknown to Charles as he had neglected to reconnoiter beforehand. In broad daylight, with clear fields of fire, the Scots

Above left: Although the rebellion failed, Lord George Murray was a great asset to the Bonnie Prince. Above right: The Duke of Cumberland turned twenty-five the day before Culloden. Though he served another twenty years, he never won another battle. Below: After his rebellion failed, Bonnie Prince Charles escaped to the Continent, where he died in exile in 1788.

would suffer terribly as they struggled across the waterlogged ground and were fired upon by English musketeers. In other words, Charles chose for battle a time and place that doomed his 5,000 soldiers from the start.

By midday on April 16, 1746, Cumberland reached Culloden with about nine thousand men. Shortly thereafter he began an advance on the Scottish line, which was drawn up on a low hill. Halting within 300 yards (273m) of the Scots, the English artillery opened a lively barrage. With their handful of guns quickly silenced, the rebels suffered greatly (and unnecessarily) for about thirty minutes as they were systematically pounded by Cumberland's cannon. Why Charles hesitated to order an attack is unclear, but by the time he finally directed his men forward, the troops had been goaded to a fury by the cannonade.

Once unleashed, the warriors of Atholl, Stuart, Cameron, Fraser, and a dozen other Highland clans, their fatigue and hunger momentarily forgotten, streamed down the gentle slope, howling their ancient battle cries. Bagpipes wailing, the clansmen lost whatever rudimentary military discipline had been drummed into them by the prince's staff over the preceding months; regiments dissolved into mobs, muskets were flung away, and

Highlanders drew their claymores (large, double-edged swords) as they ran. Wet ground canalized the charge toward the British left, further disordering the Scots while packing them closely together.

In contrast, the British below waited silently in their scarlet ranks, muskets ready. Batteries pirouetted neatly and were brought to bear against the onrushing clans. Canister steadily tore into the Scottish flank from Cumberland's center. The English regiments facing Charles's attack allowed the wild-eyed clansmen to approach within 30 yards (27.3m) before firing. The effect was devastating. Surviving Highlanders had to clamber over mounds of bodies three or four deep to reach their foes. The check to their impetus allowed the British to redouble their fire—two regimental cannon cut loose just as the Highlanders came within arm's reach.

A few hundred Scots survived the massacre to break through Cumberland's first line, and two English regiments were forced briefly into hand-to-hand combat, where the Scottish swordsmen had the advantage; the outcome, though, was never in doubt. The Highlanders who penetrated the English line were trapped and annihilated by supporting battalions. The rest began to stumble back toward their own lines, their spirit broken. As the defeat of the clans became evident, Cumberland immediately shifted from defense to offense. A few isolated Scottish units offered resistance, but the majority of Bonnie Prince Charles's army, asked to do too much for too long, simply melted away toward the sheltering highlands.

Charles should not be criticized for boldness. He faced long odds, and in such situations calculated risks are often the only way to gain victory. But the Young Pretender allowed either desperation or blind faith in his army's fighting spirit to convince him that the gamble at Culloden was an acceptable one. It was not, and Charles's foolish choice of ground did nothing to lower the odds. As a result, at the price of about 300 casualties, versus 1,500 or so Scottish, England subdued the Highland clans forever.

◆　◆　◆

An interesting counterpoint to Culloden took place a decade later in the New World, at a time when faith in firepower was reaching its peak in Europe. A regular British force, product of the same discipline and training that crippled the clans, met its fate on ground that was highly unsuitable for European-style warfare and at the hands of an army that was more than half tribal. The victors in this case, however, cleverly turned Europe's own weapons against her.

This 1746 woodcut vividly illustrates the destruction of the Scottish clans at Culloden. Few soldiers of the British second or third lines even fired their weapons. The Duke of Cumberland rides in the right foreground.

Monongahela

The men from what storys they had heard of the Indians in regard to their scalping and Mahawking, were so pannick struck that their officers had little or no command over them, and if any got a shott at one the fire immediately ran through ye whole line though they saw nothing but trees....

—Anonymous British officer

In the summer of 1755, a column of British regulars led by Major General Edward Braddock and supplemented by Maryland, North Carolina, and Virginia colonials (including a young American lieutenant colonel named George Washington), pushed through the wilds of Pennsylvania. The tiny band of some 1,400 men and 15 artillery pieces was bent on evicting the French garrison at Fort Duquesne, in the latest round of the seemingly endless Anglo-French contest over who would control the territories of North America. Cutting a road through the thick forest as they went, Braddock's men had traversed 115 miles (184km) of wilderness in twenty-four days, but the march had been well conducted and uneventful. Now, on the morning of July 9, only one obstacle remained between them and the French fort: the shallow Monongahela River.

Expecting the French to block the crossing, Braddock dispatched an advance guard under Lieutenant Colonel Thomas Gage to clear the far bank. The British, peering apprehensively into the surrounding woods, cau-

Fort Dequesne, the future site of Pittsburgh, was the goal of the British column under General Edward Braddock (above left). The English stumbled into French defenders just south of a large clearing in the Pennsylvania woods.

tiously splashed across, moved up the bank, and established themselves on the other side. To their mingled relief and amazement, they found no Frenchmen opposing them.

The French, in fact, should have been there. Fort Duquesne was only 8 miles (12.8km) away, and the ford offered an excellent defensive position. But the French commander had been caught unawares by the proximity of the British, and the blocking force he sent out under Captain de Beaujeu, consisting of 108 French regulars, 146 Canadian militia, and 600 Indians, arrived just after the British vanguard secured the far side. The two sides clashed almost immediately.

De Beaujeu fell at once, the Canadian militia fled in panic at the first volley, and the Indians, for the most part, began to melt back into the undergrowth. At this point, Lieutenant Colonel Gage should have pushed forward into a nearby clearing that would have allowed the British some maneuvering space or shifted sideways to a small hill just off the trail; either tack promised an easy victory. Instead, he stood his ground, and this

small mistake had tragic consequences. Given a brief respite, French officers managed to rally the Indians, who spread out around the British vanguard, occupying the high ground and using the abundant cover as shelter from the English fire.

Braddock's position at this point was not really dangerous; if he had scouted carefully, deployed his troops to sweep the woods on either flank, and moved ahead deliberately, he probably could have rolled up the French and Indian force fairly easily. Instead, confused by the sudden unexpected rattle of musketry, he rushed ahead to the advance guard. The rest of the column, left to its own devices, naturally followed over the river, just as Gage pulled back to escape the enemy's flanking fire. As a result, the two parts of the British force collided. Braddock, Washington, and Gage tried to clear the resultant confusion, but to no avail. The American militiamen either bolted

or hunkered down amid the underbrush and the British regulars flailed the woods with volleys and grapeshot. But the French skirmishers and the Indians cunningly used the terrain to avoid the worst of the fire. At the same time their shots could hardly miss, as the redcoats, struggling to sort themselves out, were tightly packed together. In desperation and at great cost, the British conducted isolated charges to force back their tormentors; this worked temporarily, but the French and Indians simply worked their way back through shallow gullies to new firing positions.

To cap the disaster, the officer in charge of the remaining artillery and wagons also moved up, firmly wedging the pieces against the British rear and rendering them useless. Braddock roared back and forth like a madman, but by this time most of his troops were no longer responsive to command. Hemmed in by an invisible enemy, sur-

A mortally wounded Braddock recrosses the Monongahela River in the wake of his shattered army.

rounded by growing numbers of dead and piteously moaning wounded, their worst nightmares of brightly painted savages materializing before their eyes, the British and American forces panicked. Small groups began to break away from the mass, and jumpy soldiers often shot their own comrades. The French and Indians, sensing victory, pressed their advantage. Shortly after his fifth horse of the day was killed, Braddock received a mortal wound and had to be carted off the field. The wreck of his army followed, with only 500 soldiers escaping unscathed. The retreat ended at a small British camp some 50 miles (80km) back down the road so laboriously built just a few days before.

Braddock's mistakes were minor ones—really only momentary lapses in

3

AUSTERLITZ • THE RETREAT FROM MOSCOW • BALACLAVA • CHANCELLORSVILLE • GETTYSBURG

The Age of Mass Armies

The Napoleonic Wars, which spanned more than two decades, from 1792 to 1815, proved to be a watershed in the history of warfare. Although the musket and the cannon had not improved significantly since the early 1700s, armies had grown much larger. In the mid-eighteenth century, field armies averaged between 30,000 and 50,000 men; by 1805 it was not unusual for an army on campaign to number 150,000 or more. Larger armies, inspirited by political or nationalist ideology, allowed commanders to substitute enthusiasm for discipline, shock power for firepower, and reckless maneuvering for precision drill. Battlefields also expanded—at Austerlitz, for example, the field was more than 5 miles (8km) long—blurring the distinction between tactics and strategy. A commander could no longer see the entire battle unfold from a single vantage point, and because of this, his ability to plan beforehand, to communicate this plan to his subordinates, to position himself at the critical point (the location from which the commander can best influence the battle, which might be on a hill overlooking the battlefield, standing with the reserve, or at the front of the army),

and to react to unforeseen emergencies became of primary importance. Successful commanders also had to develop nerves of steel, since so many vital developments took place outside their field of vision.

Blunders during the Age of Mass Armies were due primarily to commanders lacking one or more of the above qualities. These leaders' failures were failures of the imagination, stemming from an inability to visualize what was happening offstage, so to speak.

The undisputed master of the era of mass warfare was a wiry, intense Corsican named Napoleon Bonaparte. Parlaying military success during France's Revolutionary Wars into political power, he made himself emperor of an aroused France in 1804. Harnessing the magnificent army he had inherited to do his bidding, Napoleon nearly succeeded in dominating Europe because he understood the possibilities inherent in mass warfare in a way his adversaries, at least initially, did not. He ultimately failed because he transgressed the limitations of mass warfare. Thus Napoleon became both beneficiary and instigator of some of the more spectacular blunders in military history.

Opposite: In this famous painting by Meissonier, Napoleon, astride his white horse, leads his Grande Armée into yet another of his more than sixty battles.

Austerlitz

One sharp blow and the war's over.

—Napoleon Bonaparte

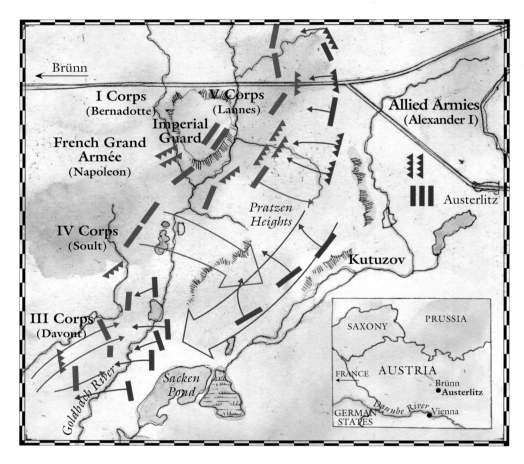

Napoleon's first campaign as emperor was, in many ways, his greatest. In the early part of 1805, Napoleon was poised to invade England, but when the Austrian and Russian empires declared war on the French he hustled his troops eastward. After his brilliant maneuvering secured a nearly bloodless triumph at Ulm, where 30,000 Austrians surrendered to the French in October, Napoleon pushed rapidly down the Danube and seized Vienna in November. Meanwhile, the Austrians and their Russian allies backpedaled into Moravia, finally pausing around the fortress of Olmütz.

From Vienna, the French emperor pursued his quarry northward, but logistical difficulties prompted him to stop at Brünn, just short of Olmütz. His ragged troops had marched more than 600 miles (960km) in just under three months, and the exhausted Grande Armée suffered shortages of everything from food to overcoats. Sickness, desertion, casualties, and the need to man numerous posts along the line of communications had reduced the size of his army from 200,000 soldiers to about 65,000. The Austrians and Russians, in contrast, received fresh infusions of manpower almost daily in the form of either scattered detachments of Austrians or reinforcements directly from Russia. By November 22, the Russo-Austrian army, commanded by Russian general Mikhail Kutuzov, numbered 80,000. Ten thousand additional troops were awaiting orders in neighboring Bohemia, while Austrian archduke Charles was pushing through Hungary with another 90,000. Finally,

Czar Alexander I (above left) planned to cut Napoleon off from his base at Brünn by sweeping around the French right. In doing so, however, he denuded his center.

the possibility existed that adroit diplomacy might entice the Prussians, who had so far remained neutral, to enter the war. All Napoleon's enemies needed was time to gather together a truly overwhelming force, time to allow Napoleon's miserable, starving troops to wither in the harsh Moravian winter, and time to complete the strategic encirclement of the Corsican upstart.

But Czar Alexander I, the unstable young ruler of the Russian empire, was in no mood to wait. Encouraged by court cronies, Alexander fancied himself the equal of Napoleon, and he eagerly desired a chance to best the French emperor in battle. Kutuzov, an old warhorse who had won his spurs in campaigns against the Turks, counseled caution, but Alexander and his fellow monarch Francis, the Austrian emperor, dismissed his arguments as defeatist maunderings.

Napoleon did everything he could to encourage Alexander's natural aggressiveness. He coyly asked for preliminary talks toward a possible truce, then staged scenes of disorder and incipient panic in his camp when Russo-Austrian negotiators arrived. He then ordered the leading elements of his army to pull back in feigned disorder and abandon the Pratzen Heights, which lay just west of Austerlitz and dominated the countryside for miles. Napoleon hoped that by creating this illusion of weakness he would lure Alexander into a decisive battle—his only chance for extricating the Grande Armée from its strategic predicament. All the while, he secretly concentrated his corps along the Goldbach, an insignificant stream about a mile (1.6km) beyond the western foot of the Pratzen, and called urgently for reinforcements in Vienna to join him.

His confidence enhanced by Napoleon's apparent weaknesses and the arrival of the Russian Imperial Guard, Alexander ordered an advance from Olmütz, with a view to crushing the Grande Armée. On November 27, 89,000 men of the Russo-Austrian army moved out on the road to Brünn. By midday on December 1, they occupied the vacant Pratzen Heights and looked down on the French waiting on the other side. After examining the enemy lines, Kutuzov's chief of staff, the Austrian Feldmarschall Leutnant Franz Ritter von Weyrother, drew up a plan for the next day. According to this plan, the Russian right would pin Napoleon's left along the Olmütź-Brünn road, then four massive columns would debouch from the Pratzen, crush the thinly held French right and encircle the entire French army from that flank. Only a small reserve was to be retained on the Pratzen. This proved to be false economy of manpower with tragic consequences.

At 1:00 A.M. on December 2, Weyrother laid out his plan for the Russian and Austrian comman-ders. Kutuzov, annoyed with the czar and childlishly determined to play no part in his army's upcoming battle, dozed through the conference. Many of the other generals present had trouble following Weyrother's pedantic presentation, partly because of language difficulties and partly because of the plan's complexity. Most returned to their armies disgruntled and apprehensive. Furthermore, the written order had to be translated from German into Russian, and because this process was not completed until very late, some officers did not receive their copies until after the battle had begun. And once they perused the order, comprising several sheets and filled with unfamiliar names of villages, forests, and streams, many commanders remained confused—few had maps of the battlefield.

On the Pratzen, the four attack columns bumped and jostled one another in the dark, becoming intermixed or lost, while harried staff officers struggled to direct them into position for the morning's attack. The chaos, which was apparent to even the rawest conscripts, dampened the soldiers' spirits, which rose only a little with the arrival of dawn and the jaunty Alexander. Finally, around 9:00 A.M., with the field

Left: Czar Alexander I on the day of battle. The twenty-eight-year-old czar considered himself Napoleon's equal as a commander. Above: Mikhail Larionovich Kutuzov. Fat, blind in one eye, petulant, and nearly sixty, he harbored few illusions about his ability to beat Napoleon.

covered by a dense fog and one column still out of place, three of the four columns stepped off toward disaster.

These three formations, consisting of about 33,000 men, soon assaulted the French positions along the Goldbach. Though the Russo-Austrian army significantly outnumbered the 12,000 French under Marshal Louis Davout opposing them, the combined forces ran into trouble almost immediately. Only the first few ranks of each column could fire upon the enemy; the remainder of the attacking host were helpless bystanders. The French, however, could hardly miss the huge, closely packed Russian and Austrian formations. The dense fog and the confusion generated by Weyrother's plan also hindered both cooperation between the columns and independent maneuvering by subordinates. The columns simply pushed ahead doggedly into the tangle of vineyards, walled parks, and solidly built villages that lined the Goldbach, hoping to break through by sheer weight of numbers.

Behind the mired Russo-Austrian left, meanwhile, the French emperor was closing a carefully laid trap. He had purposefully stripped his right in order

to concentrate a carefully concealed striking force in the low ground behind his center. As the attack on the Goldbach began, Napoleon sent this mass toward the denuded Pratzen, hoping to smash the enemy's center. Cloaked by fog, two French corps reached the foot of the Pratzen before Kutuzov, having querulously absented himself from the main attack, chanced to notice them. Shaken from his black mood, the Russian commander whipped the laggard fourth column and the Imperial Guard into a hasty defensive line. But the Russians could not withstand the furious onrush of the French, and after a sharp fight the entire Pratzen was in Napoleon's hands.

As if on cue, the sun parted the mist cloaking the field, revealing the French swarming over the Pratzen. Too late, the Russian and Austrian commanders leading the attack on the Goldbach realized their predicament. Stymied by the tenacious French defense, their armies could not go forward. French artillery on the Pratzen blocked retreat to the east, and enemy infantry

columns were already snaking their way down the backside of the heights. The only possible means of escape lay to the south, but even this route was partially blocked by streams and frozen ponds. Some of the Russian and Austrian soldiers managed to make their way to safety over a few narrow causeways, raked by artillery fire, but the bulk of the panic-stricken Russo-Austrian left wing was trapped and destroyed.

Total Russo-Austrian losses for the day amounted to 27,000 men, roughly one-third of the army, versus about 8,000 French. Moreover, the survivors fled in three different directions, effectively rendering the entire force *hors de combat.* As is true with any disaster of this magnitude, the blame can be apportioned to any number of persons. By forcing needless battle upon his reluctant generals, Alexander opted for the only course of action that could lead to defeat. The Russo-Austrian attack was clumsy in conception and execution, reflecting the incompetence of many of the officer corps, and Kutuzov deserves censure for abdicating his responsibilities as chief commander. Nevertheless, the key blunder was Weyrother's, who left the Pratzen Heights bare, a needless mistake that allowed Napoleon to pierce his center, dooming the Russo-Austrian forces to utter ruin.

◆ ◆ ◆

Following his victory at Austerlitz, Napoleon went on to humble most of the great powers of Europe. By 1811 only England and Russia still refused to bend to his will. Well protected by the "wooden walls" of the Royal Navy, England remained essentially invulnerable, leaving only Czar Alexander's empire as a suitable victim for Napoleon's next stroke.

Napoleon did not believe that invading Russia would be easy. He had studied far too much military history to be unaware that the country's seemingly endless infertile plains, swamps, and forests had become the graveyard of more than one invading army. Therefore, he prepared meticulously, gathering a tremendous host of more than 600,000 soldiers. Only about half of these were French; the remainder were drawn from more than a dozen French satellites and allies. The army's artillery and supply wagons, with which Napoleon's quartermasters accumulated huge stockpiles of rations throughout Poland and East Prussia, were hauled by 120,000 horses.

On June 22, 1812, Napoleon's vanguard crossed the Nieman River into Russia. For the next several months, Napoleon attempted to ensnare the Russians, but Czar Alexander I, chastened by the defeat at Austerlitz and

subsequent Russian humiliations at the hands of the master, adopted a Fabian strategy of withdrawal. (Named after a Roman general who successfully used this stratagem against Hannibal, a Fabian strategy of withdrawal is one in which a weaker army continually avoids battle with the stronger force, thus wearing down the stronger army and making it possible to turn the tables.) Each time Napoleon began to close the net around the Russian army, it slipped away to the east.

Meanwhile, each passing day made it clearer to Napoleon that he had severely underestimated the difficulties of campaigning in Russia. The torrid summer heat and the hard marching drained the strength of the Grande Armée. With crops still unready for harvesting, there was little for the troops to forage, and supply wagons rarely kept up with the hurrying columns. Hunger, dehydration, and heatstroke became constant companions on the march. By the beginning of August, at least 40,000 horses had died, further crippling the movement of supplies; at the same time, 100,000 soldiers were missing, sick, or dead—all without a single major engagement.

On September 7, Napoleon finally caught up with the main Russian army, which was commanded by Bonaparte's old Austerlitz nemesis, Kutuzov, as it

The Bridge at Spitz

Before the battle of Austerlitz, as Napoleon was still chasing the Austrians down the Danube, an incident occurred that epitomizes the differences between the French and Austrian armies. When the French arrived at the town of Spitz, they realized that the bridge over the Danube there, which was mined and guarded by a large rear detachment of Austrian grenadiers, had to be seized quickly. The two French marshals on the scene, Joachim Murat and Jean Lannes, deciding that a frontal attack was out of the question, cooked up a scheme to take the bridge by guile.

Donning their full-dress uniforms and concealing a storming party close by, the two marshals nonchalantly approached the Austrian sentries guarding the near side. The pickets fell back, loosing a wild shot or two, but the Frenchmen merely waved and called out cheerily to the astonished engineers preparing the bridge for demolition. Lannes told a flustered Austrian officer that an armistice had been signed that specifically placed the bridge in French hands, and he ordered him to withdraw his men immediately. The Austrian protested, saying that he must consult with his general first, and Lannes bade him do so.

As he hurried off, the French storming party arose from concealment and began to march double-time toward the bridge. One Austrian snatched up a firebrand to set off the explosives beneath the main span, but Lannes admonished him, warning that such an action could sabotage the armistice. Murat, meanwhile, was distracting the noncommissioned officer in charge of the guns at the far end of the bridge, who was understandably suspicious of the entire proceeding. At this point, General Auersperg, the Austrian in charge of the defenses, appeared. The two Frenchmen blathered on about an armistice as the storming party hustled up, befuddling poor Auersperg, who of course had heard of no such thing.

One of the Austrian gunners, eyeing the approaching French infantry and his bemused commander, moved to fire his gun, but Lannes sat on the barrel until his infantrymen arrived. Faced with a fait accompli, a sputtering Auersberg agreed to withdraw, leaving the vital span in French hands without a fight.

finally turned to fight before Moscow. By this time the Grande Armée had shrunk to about 130,000 weary men, a mere shadow of its former self. The rigors of the extended campaign had exhausted not only the French forces but also their emperor, and during the ensuing Battle of Borodino, Napoleon showed little of his former fire or tactical brilliance. Suffering from a severe cold and bladder problems, he launched an unimaginative and brutal frontal assault against the dug-in Russians. Though this attack opened the road to

Moscow, the French suffered 30,000 more casualties and failed to crush Kutuzov, whose beaten but intact army limped away as night fell.

The French entered Moscow on September 14. Napoleon arrived a day later. To the Grande Armée, wracked by typhus, dysentery, and hunger, and demoralized by the seemingly endless campaign, the ancient Russian capital beckoned as a haven offering full larders and shelter for the oncoming winter. But this haven proved instead to be a trap.

The Retreat From Moscow

We are granted only a limited time for making war; I give myself another six years, after which even I ought to come to a stop.

—Napoleon Bonaparte,
seven years before the invasion of Russia

Standing atop the walls of the Kremlin, Napoleon looked out over a gutted city. Fires, some of which had certainly been set by the Russian rearguard, had consumed the capital for three days. Below, the French emperor could make out bands of men rescuing what stores they could, though it would not be enough to sustain the army through the long Russian winter. The little food that had been available in the surrounding countryside was already picked clean, and hordes of cossacks hovered nearby, discouraging any longer-range foraging efforts. To complicate matters, typhus and dysentery had broken out, further cramming the already packed hospitals. Only iron discipline held together the remnants of an increasingly mutinous Grande Armée. Worst of all, despite the loss of Moscow, Czar Alexander showed no inclination to conclude an armistice. Napoleon may have mused on the irony of it all: here he stood, master of Europe from Spain to Moscow, but the moment at which his empire reached its greatest geographical extent was also the hour of his army's direst peril.

Perhaps 100,000 soldiers remained to Napoleon in the environs of the Russian capital. Another 130,000 guarded the supply line that snaked 550 miles (880km) back to Poland and was threatened by several Russian armies operating against its flanks. Kutuzov, after abandoning Moscow, had withdrawn southwest to the city of Kaluga, where he now had assembled 110,000 men. The condition of the

Above: At Maloyaroslavets, Napoleon was deflected from the southerly route of retreat he had planned. Left: By 1812, Napoleon had been at war for nearly twenty years. Physically, he was worn out; the strain had also dulled his power of judgment.

Grande Armée, the approaching winter, and the strategic situation left Napoleon no choice: he had to retreat from Moscow.

Like a scourge of locusts, the French troops had stripped bare the Russian countryside along their route to the capital. To return along the same path meant starvation. Napoleon therefore planned to return to Poland along a more southerly route, through untouched provinces where food could still be obtained. Accordingly, he abandoned Moscow on October 19, and headed for Kaluga.

The Battle of New Orleans

The Napoleonic Wars were not confined to Europe. Fighting more or less related to Bonaparte's wars of conquest also raged in the Americas, Africa, and Asia. This included the War of 1812, in which the still young United States tried to take advantage of Britain's distraction to invade Canada and enforce the principle of freedom of the seas. Unfortunately for the former colonials, the British quite handily defeated the Americans in virtually every land battle, even burning their capitol in 1814. The Battle of New Orleans, however, was a resounding American victory.

On January 8, 1815, 8,000 men under Lieutenant General Sir Edward Pakenham, a distinguished veteran of the Napoleonic Wars, prepared to sweep aside a motley assortment of troops under the American commander, Andrew Jackson. Jackson's army, which numbered fewer than 6,000, included raw militiamen, a battalion of African-American troops, a group of patriots from the backwoods of Tennessee, and even pirates led by the legendary Jean Lafitte. Though small and disorganized, this army was well entrenched along the Mississippi River, guarding the southern approaches to New Orleans. Pakenham, disdainful of American martial abilities, ordered a frontal assault. His soldiers marched into a leaden maelstrom; the Americans might not have been able to match the English on the parade field, but they were certainly quality marksmen. Their volleys tore huge gaps in Pakenham's lines, and the few elements that reached the American defensive works were soon driven back. Pakenham died trying to rally one of his regiments as it quailed in the face of American firepower. Before night fell, the British suffered 2,057 casualties, and withdrew from the field. The Americans experienced only 71 casualties, just 13 of which were deaths.

It is probably just as well that Pakenham died that day, for he was spared a final ironic indignity. As his body was being packed in a cask of rum for return to England, news arrived that British and American diplomats had signed a peace treaty on Christmas Eve, 1814, two weeks before the Battle of New Orleans.

Left: A French staff officer goes down beneath cossack lances at Maloyaroslavets. The sacrifice of his staff and escort allowed the emperor to make a narrow escape. Below: The Grande Armeé retreats from Moscow. In the foreground, stragglers strip the dead, scavenge for food, and burn wagons for warmth.

On October 24, a tough battle developed over a seemingly minor objective: a bridge over the Lusha River at the town of Maloyaroslavets. After much seesaw fighting, the French advance guard succeeded in carving out a tenuous bridgehead. Later that afternoon the Russians withdrew to lick their wounds, leaving only a screening force (a very thin line of troops whose only function is to keep an eye on the enemy) to observe the French. The emperor, who arrived after the action had come to a close, was reluctant to have the bulk of the Grande Armée cross the bridge, as he was afraid the Russians might return in force.

The next day, Napoleon crossed to the south bank to make a personal reconnaissance. As he rode along, a band of cossacks suddenly topped the ridge that ran along the southern edge of Maloyaroslavets, and Napoleon's staff briefly defended their emperor before reinforcements arrived to drive off the ambushers. This apparently trivial skirmish led to momentous consequences. A shaken Napoleon (he afterward carried a bag of poison around his neck to use in case of capture) hurried back across the bridge, convinced that Kutuzov was merely trying to lure him over the river, and ordered the army to turn around. Forsaking any attempt to reach the unspoiled country around Kaluga, the Grande Armée would instead return to Poland along the same devastated route it had traveled to get to Moscow.

This incredible blunder, born of despair, confusion, and fear, was so out of character for the normally brilliant Napoleon that historians still wonder at it. Had the emperor proceeded forward to the ridge that blocked his view southward, or even if he had simply ordered some reconnaissance in that direction, he would have discovered that Kutuzov had in fact abandoned any attempt to stop the French from making a safe retreat. The road to Kaluga—and to salvation for the Grande Armée—lay wide open. But instead of taking that road, Napoleon

sentenced his troops to a slow and painful death along the road home.

Thoroughly disheartened, the Grande Armée retraced its steps. It passed over the battlefield at Borodino, where wolves gnawed the carcasses of 30,000 unburied soldiers, a daunting portent of things to come. As food quickly gave out, weakened soldiers abandoned their muskets or joined the horde of stragglers following in the army's wake. Soon, as march discipline broke down, the column stretched almost 50 miles (80km); thousands of horses were slaughtered for their flesh, resulting in the abandonment of artillery and wagons, which often were loaded with wounded soldiers. Bands of cossacks harried the remnants of the French army and peasant guerrillas mercilessly dispatched those who became separated from the main body. Whenever a depot was reached, such as the one at Smolensk, it was discovered that ravenous looters had despoiled it, and the soldiers would trudge on with empty bellies.

By November 9, the Grande Armée had only forty thousand soldiers who remained fit enough to bear arms. That evening, the first snow fell, and bitter cold was added to the miseries that afflicted Napoleon's men. Additionally, regular Russian forces began a series of maneuvers to cut the road, forcing the Grande Armée time and again to fight their way through roadblocks at great cost. As the winter deepened, Napoleon's army stumbled numbly back, leaving at every step another corpse swiftly shrouded by snow.

At last, on December 11, the leading elements of the French army recrossed the Nieman. Only 7,000 soldiers remained with the colors (present for duty and ready to fight as an organized body of troops), with perhaps another 20,000 emaciated stragglers drifting along behind. Napoleon was already riding hard for Paris to raise fresh troops, but his blunder at Maloyaroslavets could not be rectified. The road he chose back from Moscow led not just to Poland, but also to Waterloo—and the end of his empire.

❖ ❖ ❖

About thirty years after Napoleon's disastrous retreat from Moscow, there occurred the most famous military blunder of the Western world, the Charge of the Light Brigade. Celebrated in literature, art, and cinema, this debacle took place during a little-known war in a remote corner of the Russian Empire. Its military significance was nil, only a relative handful of men were involved, and unlike most of the battles examined here, no kingdom's fate depended upon the outcome. Nevertheless, no study of military blunders would be complete without paying tribute to the combination of bravery, devotion to duty, and stupidity that made the Charge of the Light Brigade possible.

The causes of the Crimean War, which pitted Russia against the odd alliance of Britain, France, and the Ottoman Empire, are so convoluted as to almost defy description. What began as a Russo-Turkish war in 1853 expanded when a horrified England contemplated the prospect of Russia's Black Sea fleet steaming unimpeded past Constantinople and into the Mediterranean. England declared war on Russia in March 1854, then joined France in sending an expeditionary force to support the Turks.

Allied strategy revolved around the capture of Sevastopol, Russia's primary naval base on the Black Sea. Consequently, in September 1854, British, French, and Turkish troops landed on the Crimean peninsula. Included among them was the British Brigade of Light Cavalry, commanded by Lord Cardigan. After a few tough battles with the Russians, the allies sealed off Sevastopol in early October. Lord Cardigan's brigade found itself encamped at the southern end of the siege works, near the minor port of Balaclava.

For a week or more, allied artillery battered away at Sevastopol's formidable defenses. Then, on October 25, the Russians sallied forth from their walls to pry open the southern end of the

The allied fleet outside the besieged fortress-port of Sevastopol.

siegeworks and destroy the base at Balaclava. The Russians advanced nearly 5 miles (8 km), overrunning a battery of British artillery and brushing aside several regiments of Turks, before they were halted just over a mile (1.6km) from Balaclava by a hard-hitting British counterattack. As the Russians fell back to a long, low ridge known as the Causeway Heights, the British commander, Lord Raglan, saw an opportunity to seal the victory. The Light Brigade sat in reserve on the western end of the ridge—a vigorous charge on their part would take the disordered enemy in the flank and recapture the British guns on the heights. Raglan hurriedly dispatched an aide to Lord Lucan, the cavalry division commander, carrying the order that propelled five British regiments to everlasting glory.

Balaclava

Men, it is a mad-brained trick, but it is no fault of mine.

—Lord Cardigan

Lord Lucan looked up from the flimsy, hastily penciled message. Next to him, Captain Lewis Edward Nolan, Raglan's aide, fidgeted with impatience. Nolan, having watched the battle at Raglan's side, understood that time was of the essence—the Russians on the heights could not be allowed to reorganize. He also considered Lucan a fussy incompetent; in fact, during a minor skirmish weeks before the two had clashed when Nolan openly criticized Lucan's handling of his division. For his part, Lucan thought of Nolan as a conceited prig, bordering on insubordinate in his lack of respect for senior officers. Lucan carefully reread the order:

> *Lord Raglan wishes the cavalry to advance rapidly to the front—follow the enemy and try to prevent the enemy carrying away the guns. Troop Horse Artillery may accompany. French cavalry is on your left. Immediate.*

"Attack, sir? Attack what? What guns, sir?" Lucan asked Nolan querulously. Unknown to either Nolan or Raglan, Lucan had neglected his duties as field commander and had not followed the battle. From where he stood, he could not see the top of the Causeway Heights or their southern side, and so was completely ignorant of the situation. The only guns visible were some Russian batteries at the far end of the valley north of the heights.

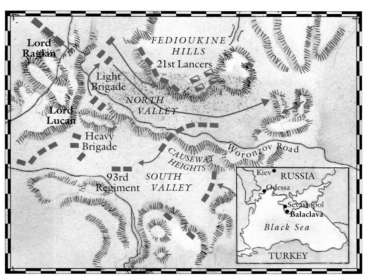

Although Lord Raglan could plainly see the top of the Causeway Heights, Lord Lucan could not—a fatal difference in perspective.

To Nolan, the question merely offered further proof of Lucan's ineptitude. He flung his arm contemptuously outward, indicating vaguely the direction of the charge, virtually spitting out the challenge, "There, my lord. There is the enemy! There are your guns!" Onlookers were shocked at his manner, but Lord Lucan merely shrugged and rode over to Cardigan; incensed as he was by Nolan's behavior, he resisted the urge to indulge his fury when time was so vital. Unfortunately, Lucan had misinterpreted Nolan's gesture. The young aide undoubtedly had meant to indicate the Causeway Heights, but Lucan believed he had pointed to the Russian batteries at the end of the valley. Both men's anger had prevented them from clarifying Raglan's order, and this confusion—and the two officers' emotions—doomed the Light Brigade.

Riding over to where the soldiers of the Light Brigade were lounging by their horses, Lucan instructed Cardigan to attack forthwith. Cardigan was not the most brilliant of tacticians, to say the least, but even he was taken aback by the order. Casting a sidelong glance down the valley, he saluted his commander, saying, "Certainly, sir; but allow me to point out to you that the Russians have a battery in the valley on our front, and batteries and riflemen on both sides." This was true. The Causeway Heights to the south and a similar ridge to the north, the Fedioukine Hills, formed a straight, narrow valley devoid of cover; the slopes of both features were teeming with enemy soldiers. The far end of the valley lay more than a mile (1.6km) distant, which meant that the Light Brigade would have to pass through most of the valley at a walk to prevent the horses from being completely exhausted before they reached their objective. Even if they reached the guns and defeated the Russian forces, the brigade could not hope to hold this position without infantry support, and they would have to pass back through the gauntlet to escape.

Lucan responded quietly, "I know it, but Lord Raglan will have it." What passed unspoken between the two was the understanding that the brigade would be destroyed. Nothing could save Cardigan and his men once they entered the valley. Then Lucan added a phrase that has prefaced many a military disaster: "We have no choice but to obey." (This debacle was immortalized in the British poet Tennyson's "The Charge of the Light Brigade," in which Lucan's sentiment became "Theirs not to reason why/Theirs but to do and die.") With this, Cardigan saluted once more and cantered over to his officers.

Within a short time the Light Brigade was formed up and moving eastward. Deployed in three lines with Lord Cardigan riding imperturbably at their head, the brigade was a beautiful sight. The brightly colored uniforms of the 11th and 8th Hussars, heavily festooned with braid, the flashing helmets of the 4th and 13th Light Dragoons, and the pennants snapping smartly from the bobbing lances of the 17th Lancers all contributed to an impres-

sion of parade-ground precision that was remarked upon by witnesses on both sides.

Murmurs of approval soon gave way to cries of horror as Lord Raglan and his staff realized that the Light Brigade was not headed toward the Causeway Heights, but down the valley. Battle-hardened officers wept and shouted futilely as they watched Cardigan leading his men to certain destruction. Captain Nolan, who had decided to join the charge, obviously realized about this time that Lord Raglan's orders had been misinterpreted. Spurring his horse ahead, he rode across the brigade's front, waving his saber and shouting something that could not be heard above the pounding of hooves. Before he could reach Cardigan to redirect the charge, how-

ever, one of the first Russian shells aimed at the British horsemen sent a shard through his heart, killing him instantly. It was poetic justice, perhaps, that Nolan should be the first to die in the charge, but his death stilled the only voice that might have saved the brigade.

Nolan's death marked the beginning of a passage through hell. With every step farther into the valley, the brigade came within range of more enemy rifles and other guns. Shells began to explode among the ranks while fire from smaller arms sang over-

This painting by Christoper Clark depicts the culmination of the charge, as the Light Brigade carves its way through the Russian battery.

head. For the first five minutes or so, Cardigan's brigade maintained its stately pace, with officers constantly correcting alignments and cautioning the men to fight their natural (and understandable) urge to hurry ahead. As casualties mounted, regiments stoically closed to the center to mend gaps torn in their ranks.

By the time the brigade had reached the halfway point, there was no restraining the men. Raked from three sides, most troopers thought of little else except escaping the trap they found themselves in. Despite the officers' best efforts, the regiments broke into a gallop, plunging toward the Russian batteries belching fire and smoke at the end of the valley.

The field became a pandemonium of noise, explosions, dust, and smoke.

The second and third lines swerved to avoid trampling the wounded, causing their formations to lose cohesion as they thundered forward. Riderless horses dashed back and forth, eyes bulging with terror, often seeking to rejoin the line as they had been trained to do. Some men remained upright in the saddle after being killed, their mounts carrying them along as though reluctant to abandon their mates even in death. Through it all, the survivors, spattered with the blood and gore of their compatriots, forged ahead, some shouting "View haloo!" as though the whole nightmare was nothing more than a gigantic fox hunt.

When the surviving English troops came within a hundred yards (90m) of the battery, the Russians fired their last salvo, and the front ranks of the Light Brigade simply disappeared—but succeeding waves overran the guns, cutting down the gunners without mercy, at last having found an enemy at whom they could strike back. The fight among the guns lasted only a few moments, and as the cavalry burst out of the smoke-shrouded battery, they discovered a new threat. Hordes of Russian cavalry were stationed just behind the now silent artillery line, and the surviving British officers frantically rallied their men to face them.

But the Russians had no stomach to face men who had just accomplished the impossible. Instead, they merely watched the shattered remnants of the brigade cautiously pick its way westward toward safety, through the debris of battle. Back through the gauntlet of fire they went—small groups of disheveled riders, others on foot, many wounded—with the Russians following carefully, callously dispatching those stragglers they were able to catch. Twenty minutes after it had begun, the charge was over.

Of the 673 soldiers who took part in this doomed maneuver, only 195 could be mustered immediately afterward—247 were killed or wounded; the remainder had been captured or were still making their way back while dodging cossack patrols. Amazingly, Lord Cardigan, who led the charge and was

the first man into the Russian battery, emerged without a scratch. All in all, this attack was a small affair of no great significance—except, of course, for those involved—that had little effect on the outcome of the war. And yet, the grotesque combination of stupidity, futile sacrifice, happenstance, bravery, and blind obedience that produced the Charge of the Light Brigade continues to fascinate professional and armchair historians nearly 150 years later.

The second great war of the Age of Mass Armies, which began seven years after the English fiasco at Balaclava, took place in North America when the United States was split in two and resorted to arms to settle various thorny constitutional issues. Though the most visible issue was whether slavery should continue to exist, the issues that divided the young republic into the Union (the North) and the Confederacy (the South) were many and varied. During the American Civil War, the weapons employed were of an order of magnitude more lethal than those used in the Napoleonic Wars; the primary example of these was the rifled musket, which granted marksmen greatly increased range and accuracy. Massed columns and grand cavalry charges, rarely employed and even less often successful, became obsolete, though the battlefield remained generally recognizable to an officer of the Napoleonic age. And despite the integration of the telegraph, the railroad, and the steam engine as essential tools of communication and transportation, Napoleon himself would have grasped the operational and strategic problems associated with the first half of the war.

Indeed, both Union and Confederate generals attempted to emulate Napoleon in their battle plans—each time they engaged the enemy, they sought to destroy him in a single climactic battle, and so end the war. In 1863, within the space of a single summer, two generals, one from each side, had the opportunity to do just that. Both fumbled the chance.

Chancellorsville

My God, my God! What will the country say?
What will the country say?

—Abraham Lincoln, on receiving news of Hooker's
defeat at Chancellorsville

"The rebel army," boasted General Joseph "Fighting Joe" Hooker to reporters gathered around him at his headquarters, "is now the legitimate property of the Army of the Potomac. They may as well pack up their haversacks and make for Richmond." Hooker's ebullient mood was understandable; he had successfully outflanked Robert E. Lee, the commander in chief of the Confederate Army, and now stood poised to crush the Army of Northern Virginia, possibly bringing the two-year-old war to an end.

The entire campaign up to this point had run like clockwork. In late April of 1863, Hooker had faced Lee across the Rappahannock River at Fredericksburg, Virginia. As Lee's position was too strong for a frontal assault, even though the Army of the Potomac outnumbered his army 94,000 to 53,000, Hooker devised a brilliant plan to entrap the rebel army. He would take 54,000 men in four corps on a long flanking march to the west, cross the Rappahannock and its tributary the Rapidan, and descend on Lee's rear. Meanwhile, 40,000 troops under Major General John Sedgwick would remain behind at Fredericksburg, ostentatiously preparing for an attack so as to deceive Leè about Hooker's true intentions. The only real obstacle was the Wilderness, a tangled, swampy

When Hooker hesitated before Chancellorsville, Lee daringly split his army into three parts—the first to keep an eye on Sedgewick, the second to contain Hooker, and the third, under Stonewall Jackson, to strike Hooker's open right flank.

stretch of overgrown forest on the south bank of the Rappahannock that Hooker would have to pass through on his way to Lee.

Had the rebels made a determined stand in the Wilderness, Hooker's timetable might have been thrown off enough to allow Lee's army to escape—but there had been only minimal resistance, and by April 30 the Union Army was encamped on the edge of the Wilderness, prepared to break out into open country the next day. Lee, apparently, was still sitting placidly at

Fredericksburg, unaware of the danger looming behind him. For all intents and purposes, Hooker had backed the Army of Northern Virginia into a corner. Should it turn to face Hooker, Sedgwick could strike; should Lee split his forces, he would be badly outnumbered on both fronts and be easily defeated; if Lee tried to withdraw, he would have Hooker striking the flank of his retreating columns while Sedgwick hammered his rear. There was no way Fighting Joe could fail, unless he lost his nerve—which is exactly what he did during the long dark hours between dusk on April 30 and dawn on May 1.

Lying alone in the dark, Hooker let his fears get the best of him. After all, he did not know where exactly Lee was. The one flaw in his plan had been to send his cavalry off on a raid against Lee's supply lines. This left him with no

scouts to search out the location of the rebels. As far as Hooker knew, Lee was still waiting complacently behind his fortifications at Fredericksburg, but who knew what scheme the masterful Confederate general might have cooked up to rescue himself and his troops from their predicament? Though each of Hooker's wings alone was a match for the Army of Northern Virginia, dividing one's force in the presence of the enemy was always dangerous, a principle the West Point graduate undoubtedly had drummed into him in many a classroom.

When Hooker arose the next morning, all his confidence of the night before had been leached away by worry. It is said that Hooker swore off alcohol for the duration of the war; it might have been beneficial for the Union cause if he had fortified his courage that morning with a stiff shot of whiskey.

Meanwhile, as planned, the Union army emerged from the Wilderness and headed east into open, rolling farmland. Around noon, they ran into Confederate opposition. Lee, detecting Hooker's movement as early as April 29, had opted to split his own force, leaving a bare 10,000 soldiers to oppose Sedgwick while rushing to meet Hooker's main force with just more than 40,000 men. The Union commanders deployed their corps, anticipating only slight difficulty in opening the way. Before they could come to grips with the rebels, however, they received the stunning order to pull back into the Wilderness, where they were to dig in and await a Confederate attack. Several corps commanders remonstrated with Hooker, but he was adamant. By late afternoon, a dispirited Union army was busily digging trenches and rifle pits among the thickets of the Wilderness. Even though he had anticipated this rebel move in his planning, the appearance of Robert E. Lee in the flesh was too much for Hooker's shaky nerves. Surely, he reasoned, the Confederate commander must have some trick up his sleeve. How else could he dare to come against the Army of the Potomac in the face of such overwhelming odds?

In fact, Lee had no particular plan on May 1, but when Hooker pulled in his horns, it gave the rebel commander the time he needed to come up with one. That evening, he and the peerless tactician Thomas "Stonewall" Jackson devised a daring maneuver to drive the Union army back across the Rappahannock. Early the next morning, Lee split his army yet again, so that now he had only 14,000 facing Hooker's force, which had been swollen by reinforcements to 70,000. An army of 28,000 men under Jackson swung wide around the right flank of the Army of the Potomac in a daylong march that left both rebel wings extremely vulnerable should Hooker emerge from his funk. But Fighting Joe merely spent the day inspecting his lines, making sure the fortifications were strong enough to repel any Confederate attack.

Two hours before nightfall, Jackson struck from the west and northwest against the Union line, which Hooker had positioned facing south, to repel Lee when he chose to attack. The rebels soon stove in Hooker's right and were driving through the Wilderness toward the river, until darkness and the wounding of Jackson brought an end to the fighting. The next morning, the attack was resumed while Hooker frantically pulled his army farther back toward the fords he had crossed in triumph only days before. Even now, Fighting Joe could have retrieved the situation. He still outnumbered the rebels two to one, only a fraction of his force had been engaged so far, and Lee's army remained split in half. But Hooker was whipped, at least in his mind. He had little thought but to save his army, and after several more days of confused

Opposite: General Joseph Hooker, a hard-driving general who feared making decisions. Above left: A photograph of Hooker in the field, by the famous Civil War photographer, Mathew Brady. Left: General Robert E. Lee, commander of the Army of Northern Virginia. A gentle man of quiet dignity, Lee inspired intense devotion among his soldiers.

The Death of Stonewall Jackson

If any single bullet could be said to have won the war for the North, it was the one that struck Stonewall Jackson at the moment of his greatest triumph. Ironically, it was not a Union soldier but one of Jackson's own men, an anonymous North Carolinian, who shot him down.

On the evening of May 2, 1863, with Hooker's men in full retreat from Jackson's flank attack through the Wilderness, the lean, angular Confederate pressed his men relentlessly through the gloom, determined to reach the Rappahannock and cut off the Army of the Potomac from its escape route. Moving from unit to unit, Jackson and his staff rode dangerously close to Union lines so that the general might judge for himself the tactical situation. As the group returned from one of these forays, Confederate pickets mistook them for Union cavalry in the dark and let loose a volley, shattering Jackson's left arm.

Surgeons subsequently amputated the ruined arm, but Jackson contracted pneumonia while recovering. He lingered at death's door for several days, with periods of lucidity alternating with fevered prayer and delirium. Just before he died on May 10, he sat up, shouting, "Order A.P. Hill to prepare for action! Pass the infantry to the front...." Then, leaving behind hallucinations of battle, he lay back, smiling serenely. "Let us cross over the river," he murmured, as he slipped away, "and rest under the shade of the trees."

The mortal wounding of General Jackson deprived the Confederacy of its ablest tactician, and this loss became critical when his successor failed to press home the attack on Cemetery Hill during the first day of the Battle of Gettysburg—a blunder the aggressive Jackson would never have committed.

dangers, yet never lost his head or his faith in victory. As a result, he defeated an army twice his size while inflicting upon it one-third more casualties than he suffered. But not all the credit can be given to Lee. No one played a larger role in the North's snatching defeat from the jaws of victory than the Union general Fighting Joe Hooker.

✦ ✦ ✦

For all the brilliance of Lee's tactical success in the Wilderness, the strategic situation had not changed appreciably. Despite the thrashing it had received, the Union Army was still a viable force; given time to recover, it would soon threaten Richmond again. What the South needed was a decisive victory on enemy territory to dishearten the Northern public and perhaps gain recognition from Great Britain or France. Confident in his ability to defeat the Army of the Potomac again, Lee hoped to force just such a showdown. Thus, in the wake of Chancellorsville, the Army of Northern Virginia launched an invasion of the North.

By late June of 1863, Confederate columns were advancing through the lush farmlands of Maryland and southeastern Pennsylvania, enjoying the rare chance to forage through areas untouched by war. Lee was well satisfied with their progress, and Southern morale was sky-high. The only disquieting note was the failure of Lee's cavalry commander, J.E.B. "Jeb" Stuart, to report the location of the Army of the Potomac. In fact, Stuart's own position was a mystery, as he had been out of contact for nearly a week, rampaging gleefully through the Union rear instead of collecting intelligence. Thus, Lee was feeling ahead blindly for the enemy, warning his commanders not to bring on a general engagement until the dispositions of the Union army were known.

On the first of July, a footsore rebel column from Ambrose Powell Hill's III Corps approached the little college town of Gettysburg, Pennsylvania, hoping to find a stockpile of shoes rumored to have been abandoned there. Instead, they found the Army of the Potomac.

fighting in the heavy underbrush of the Wildnerness, the Army of the Potomac disconsolately passed over to the north bank of the Rappahannock.

Few campaigns highlight so vividly the importance of the commander's will. Joseph Hooker drew up a near-perfect plan, possessed the advantages of numbers, and surprise, and came within a few miles of bringing his plan to fruition. At the last moment, though, he fell prey to self-doubt, a weakness either missing or sternly controlled in the breasts of successful commanders. On the other hand, Lee faced real, not imaginary,

Gettysburg

This has been my fight, and upon my shoulders rests the blame.

—Robert E. Lee

The Battle of Gettysburg lasted for three days. On each of the first two days, victory eluded the rebels because of the blunders of one or more of Lee's subordinates; on the final day, Lee himself turned defeat into disaster.

On the morning of July 1, the failure of Lee's cavalry commander to feed the commander in chief information about Union dispositions resulted in Hill's men colliding blindly with Union cavalry just west of Gettysburg; this in turn resulted in a fight that Lee had hoped to postpone. Despite Lee's orders to the contrary, Hill committed the bulk of his troops as they came up. Nevertheless, Lee made the best of a bad situation and ordered the concentration of his army around the sleepy Pennsylvania hamlet. The early fighting favored the rebels, and by late afternoon Confederate commander Richard Ewell's II Corps was poised to seize Cemetery Hill, the linchpin of the Union position on the high ground south of Gettysburg. Lee had strongly urged his subordinate to press the attack, but the cautious Ewell delayed the assault until his last few brigades could join him. This respite allowed the Army of the Potomac to reinforce Cemetery Hill, forcing Ewell to call off

After failing to seize Culp's Hill and Little Round Top on the second day of fighting at Gettysburg, Lee resolved to break the Union center along Cementery Ridge.

the attack. Had Ewell acted promptly, there is little doubt that the Northern army would have had to abandon the field; instead, still in possession of the high ground, and with reinforcements swelling their strength from 20,000 to nearly 80,000 troops, the Union forces prepared to continue the contest on the second day of July.

That night, Lee gently rebuked the dilatory Ewell, but his mind was already working away at the next day's maneuvers. Lee decided to attack the Union left with General James Longstreet's I Corps, while Ewell's men demonstrated on the other end of the field to distract Union reserves. Time was of the essence, for the Army of the Potomac had not yet been able to anchor its left flank on the slight eminence known as Little Round Top.

Unfortunately for the South, Longstreet's corps took five hours to get into position. The lost time proved to be the margin of defeat, as Little Round Top was occupied a scant fifteen minutes before the rebels reached it, literally as two regiments of Alabamans were scrambling up its rocky slopes. Longstreet's brigades hammered their opponents hard, and the gray-and-butternut waves lapped halfway up Little Round Top, but they could go no farther. As darkness blanketed the field a second time the rebel tide receded. The best and, unbeknownst to the combatants, the final chance for Confederate victory had slipped away.

If Lee felt discouragement, he did not show it. Although his original strength of 63,000 had dwindled to about 47,000 who were still able to fight, he considered his veterans more than a match for the numerically superior army opposing him. Furthermore, he assumed that Meade, having fought a desperate defensive battle on both wings, must have stripped his center bare. Therefore, he resolved to stake everything on a final, climactic assault the next morning, with the aim of breaking the Union line in the middle.

On July 3, Lee massed his artillery and his 12,000 infantrymen, including the fresh division of George Pickett, which would lead the charge. Preparations were accomplished as quickly and quietly as possible, so as not to attract attention, and the infantry, occupying a line a mile (1.6km) long, hunkered down behind cover to await the outcome of the preliminary bombardment. Lee expected his 140 guns to silence the Union batteries along Cemetery Ridge. Then the cream of the Army of Northern Virginia, men who had never failed him before, would crack open the Northern position, scattering the Army of the Potomac back along the road to Washington.

While Lee was almost sure this plan would work, Longstreet remained unconvinced. While examining the ground with Lee, he protested vehemently. His men would have to advance almost a mile (1.6 km) over flat, open ground in the face of entrenched infantry and under the shadow of a ridge bristling with artillery. "It is my opinion," he said, "that no 15,000 men ever arrayed for battle can take that position." As it turned out, Longstreet was right.

At 1:00 P.M. the greatest artillery barrage the continent had ever wit-

Above: General James Longstreet directs the attack on the second day of Gettysburg. Below: General George Pickett led and lent his name to the final rebel charge at Gettysburg. He never completely lived down the fact that he survived the disaster unscathed.

nessed began, but its results fell far short of Lee's hopes. Smoke and dust generated by the bombardment obscured the Union lines, so that most of the rebel shells passed harmlessly over their targets. Thus, when the barrage ended an hour later and the rebel infantry emerged from hiding, the Union guns were ready to respond.

This advance was an odd, yet stirring sight. The Southern force of 12,000 ragamuffins, clothed in threadbare uniforms supplemented haphazardly with bits of civilian clothing, many of them barefoot, marched in perfectly aligned ranks. As they passed their own artillery, the battlefield momentarily fell silent, as if both sides realized that the fate of the Union hung

on the outcome of the Confederate charge. At the rate of one hundred yards (91m) a minute, the rebels closed the wide gap between them and the Yankees. Before they had gone a quarter of the way, however, Union cannonballs began to spoil the precision of their formations. As they drew closer, carefully closing the gaps in their lines, rifle fire rang out, ineffective at first, but growing more lethal as the blue-clad infantry found its range. Artillery on all the high ground from Little Round Top to Cemetery Hill soon joined in; some guns could be fired at an angle, enabling each ball to topple a dozen men. Once the gray lines passed the halfway point, fire from 7,000 rifles and more than 100 guns were tearing at them. Regimental flags seemed to bob rhythmically as successive bearers fell and were replaced. Their hats perched atop their swords (so they could be seen more easily by the soldiers), the officers urged their men on, but the line gradually shaped itself into a wedge as the wings hesitated in the face of Union firepower. When the leading ranks began to mount the gentle slope of Cemetery Ridge, the Northern gunners switched to canister, mowing down great

The Lost Orders

The Gettysburg campaign was not Lee's first invasion of the North. That had come a year earlier, also on the heels of victory in Virginia. In 1862, however, the Army of Northern Virginia was turned back not by defeat in battle, but by carelessness.

In September 1862, Lee's army was scattered across Maryland by the South's need to capture Harper's Ferry and secure the line of communications. Lee was not particularly worried by this state of affairs, because his adversary at this time was General George McClellan, a sluggish commander whom he had bested several times before. Within a few days, Lee felt, his army could be concentrated to deal McClellan's Army of the Potomac a blow that might end the war.

But that opportunity disappeared on the afternoon of September 13. On that day, in an area recently passed through by the rebels, a Union private stumbled across three cigars wrapped in paper. Unwrapping the unexpected bounty, he noticed handwriting on the paper. As this writing appeared to be an order of some kind, the young private passed it on to his commander, who imme-

diately realized its significance. The cigar wrapping was, in fact, Special Order 191, in which the dispositions of the Army of Northern Virgina were detailed and Lee's invasion plans outlined. Within two hours the crumpled document was in the hands of McClellan, who hooted that he had the paper that would allow him to "whip Bobbie Lee." Luckily for Lee, a Confederate spy in Union headquarters alerted the rebels to the fact that their secret plans had been compromised; nevertheless, it is a measure of Lee's generalship and McClellan's incompetence that the Confederate army was subsequently able to escape from Maryland mostly intact.

Who exactly misplaced the order is unknown, though it was addressed to Daniel Harvey Hill, one of Lee's subordinate commanders. Probably a staff officer neglected to file the order properly, and in the confusion of moving Hill's headquarters, it became a convenient wrapper for someone's last few precious cigars. How they were then deposited in a Maryland field is also a mystery, but the loss of those cigars just might have lost the South the Civil War.

swathes of the world's finest infantry. Finally, the rebels' good order gave way as they stumbled forward through the hail of lead, assailed on both flanks by detached battalions of Union infantry sent out to catch the Confederate regiments in a deadly crossfire.

Lee watched all this from his command post. He saw Confederate battle flags, against all odds, break through the first Union line, tremble briefly on the ridgetop, and then fall. Shortly thereafter, the survivors began to stream back, pursued by vengeful Union fire. Lee's thoughts at this moment are unrecorded, but he responded to the failure of "Pickett's Charge" with all his considerable nobility of spirit. He moved forward to comfort the men and rally those who could still fight, assuring the weeping commanders that "your men have done all that men can do. The fault is entirely my own."

After Pickett's Charge, Lee abandoned any thoughts of invasion and withdrew from the North. Throughout the first two days of the battle, Lee had repeatedly been let down by his subordinates, though he must shoulder some of the blame for his failure to ensure that his orders were carried out promptly when timely action might have secured a decisive victory. But Pickett's Charge was his fault alone, the product of wishful thinking and over-

confidence in his beloved soldiers. Until the third day, Gettysburg had been a draw—nothing more nor less than a frustrating check for Lee. The great assault on the last day, however, crippled the Army of Northern Virginia. Of the 12,000 or so elite soldiers who participated in Pickett's Charge, 60 percent were killed, captured, or wounded. Altogether, Lee lost 28,000 infantrymen during those three summer days at Gettysburg. The battle gutted the South's premier fighting force—a mortal wound that would take two more years to kill its victim.

The American Civil War was the last great Western conflict fought almost entirely with muzzle-loading weapons. During the early battles of this war, troops in gaily colored uniforms, accompanied by bandsmen and following their regimental standards, marched into combat much as Napoleon's Grande Armée had. The War Between the States was also the first war characterized by widespread use of the railroad, the telegraph, ironclad naval vessels, and steamships. In the last year of the war, the combatants introduced the Gatling gun (a forerunner of the machine gun), heavy use of entrenchments, primitive land mines, and early versions of barbed wire. In other words, the Civil War marked both the culmina-

tion and the end of mass warfare in the old style. Weapons technology progressed so rapidly after the war that the nature of battle itself was transformed, though unfortunately for the participants, few generals of the time understood this.

After the Civil War, the United States, outside of her "splendid little war" with Spain in 1898, fought no major war until 1917. From 1871 to 1914, Europe remained mostly peaceful, the exceptions being the savage Russo-Turkish War of 1878, and a series of comic-opera wars in the Balkans from 1912 to 1913. But the soldiers of both continents were deeply engaged in subduing the other peoples of the world, during an era when colonial empires were expanding to every corner of the globe. At a time when armies had grown unmanageably large and lethal, most military professionals experienced combat in "little wars."

Opposite: The "high tide of the Confederacy." General Richard Armistead (sword raised in center) leads the survivors of Pickett's Charge onto Cemetery Ridge. Armistead was shot down as his hand touched the cannon wheel, and the rebels were driven back immediately thereafter. Above: The aftermath: rebel dead litter the field at Gettysburg.

4

LITTLE BIG HORN • ISANDHLWANA ADOWA • OMDURMAN

Colonial Warfare

During the late 1800s the major powers of Europe and the United States directed a great deal of energy toward establishing or expanding their colonial empires. Since native peoples tended to object to being colonized, this empire-building met with armed resistance almost everywhere. Colonial warfare typically pitted small contingents of Western regulars, often supplemented with local troops, against much larger, though less well-equipped, native armies.

Often outnumbered and usually isolated in alien lands, Western armies relied on superior firepower, training, and discipline to overcome their foes. Native forces, though they had inferior weaponry and equipment, were normally larger and more familiar with local conditions than the enemy; they were also inspired to great bravery, as they were defending hearth and home against unjust invasions. These factors tended to strike a fine balance, making pitched battles in colonial warfare very chancy affairs. Successful leaders, on either side, were those who perceived and exploited the imbalances inherent to the clash of different military systems. Blunderers acted upon the belief that the strengths of their army—whether sheer numbers, repeating rifles, religious fanaticism, or some other perceived advantage—would

enable them to overcome any threat the enemy might pose. In some cases they muddled through—Gatling guns could put right many a military blunder, for instance—but when they failed to do so, their men often wound up being massacred.

While Americans do not generally think of the taming of their western frontier as a colonial war, the campaigns against the native inhabitants of the vast continent that the United States laid claim to were just that; just as the British were conducting campaigns to conquer peoples and lands of the east, the U.S. government sent its army to subjugate the Native Americans. Though the fight for continental domination began in the seventeenth century and continued on until almost the twentieth, the most familiar era remains the decades after the Civil War, when soldiers in dusty outposts scattered across the American West subdued the Plains Indians. Bred in a warrior tradition that used raiding, ambush, and deception as fundamental battle tactics, the Cheyenne, Crow, Dakota, Sioux, and a dozen other Native American tribes proved to be canny and resourceful foes. Carelessness or overconfidence on the part of U.S. Army commanders often had to be paid for in blood.

Opposite: The greatest fiasco of the Battle of Omdurman was probably the charge of the British Lancers into a gully filled with 2,000 Sudanese warriors.

Little Big Horn

That man will stop at nothing. He is going to take us right into the village, where there are many more warriors than we are. We have no chance at all.

—Mitch Boyer, scout killed with Custer at Little Big Horn

Lieutenant Colonel George Armstrong Custer, peering down into the hazy valley of the Little Big Horn River on the morning of June 25, 1876, began to formulate the last military maneuver of his life. For the past few days his 7th Cavalry Regiment had been on the trail of an Indian band of unknown size, as part of a larger campaign against the Sioux and northern Cheyenne tribes in Dakota Territory. Scouting reports indicated that their camp lay ahead, along the west bank of the Little Big Horn. Custer had been assigned to drive the "hostiles" (the name U.S. Army operatives gave to resistant Native Americans) into the arms of converging columns operating in the territory ahead of him. Gathered around him now were his Indian (mainly Crow and Dakota) scouts, some bearing unfavorable news.

Custer had hoped to approach the Indian camp unseen, but Sioux outriders had detected his presence. Several of Custer's scouts placed the size of the hostile gathering at more than 7,000 men, women, and children; according to a rough rule of thumb, this meant that his 600 cavalry-men would face approximately 2,000 warriors. Custer, however, regarded these reports with some skepticism. In his opinion, the hostile band was perhaps one-third that size, and he was more concerned that it would attempt to disperse than that the warriors would stand and fight.

Therefore, Custer resolved to use the standard tactics he had developed during his ten years on the frontier. He split the 7th Cavalry into three parts. Three companies under Captain Frederick Benteen would swing to the left to reconnoiter and scoop up any fugitives from the main

Above: Separated by the Little Big Horn, Custer and Reno were defeated in detail by the Indian warriors facing them. Reno, however, dug in along the bluffs and managed to survive the battle. Left: This Brady portrait of Custer was made during the Civil War, during which Custer was promoted from lieutenant to general. After the war, along with many others, he was reduced to the rank of lieutenant colonel. Opposite: Custer's Last Stand is probably the most painted scene in American military history. This 1976 tempera painting by Gary Zaboly captures Custer organizing his final defense against the Indian onslaught.

action, rejoining the second detachment, which consisted of three companies led by Major Marcus Reno, as soon as possible. Reno's battalion would parallel the main striking force of five companies commanded by Custer himself. Reno's battalion and Custer's force would each charge the encampment from different directions to ensure that none of the hostiles could escape. Normally, Custer preferred a dawn attack, but circumstances dictated that he close with the Indians immediately, before they could melt into the surrounding countryside.

As the three columns separated, Custer noticed one of his Crow scouts, Half Yellow Face, stripping and applying ritual war paint. Half Yellow Face had urged Custer not to split his com-

mand, reiterating that the hostile band ahead was far larger than Custer assumed, but the white man had cut him short. "You do the scouting," he said, "and I will attend to the fighting." Now Custer asked the Crow why he painted himself. "Because you and I are going home today," the scout replied stoically, "and by a trail that is strange to us both."

Later that day, Reno's and Custer's columns, on opposite banks of the Little Big Horn, approached the southern end of the Indian village. Just before 3:00 P.M., approximately 500 Sioux warriors swarmed out of the village to attack Reno's 140 men. The major ordered his troopers to dismount and form a skirmish line. The Sioux soon began to edge around Reno's skirmishers, forcing

the major to pull his line back into a nearby stand of timber. The two sides exchanged shots for a time, until a scout near Reno had his head blown off. Covered in blood, Reno evidently lost his composure, issued a series of wildly contradictory orders, and finally directed his men to seek refuge on some wooded high ground across the river. Reno's panic was transmitted to his commanders, and the withdrawal became a wild scramble as jubilant Indians fired at will upon the disordered cavalry. By the time Reno gained the bluffs on the opposite bank, he had lost 45 men and was, for all intents and purposes, out of the fight.

Custer, meanwhile, observing the early stages of Reno's fight but not the retreat, hurried his command ahead,

The Guns Left Behind

Custer's last thoughts are unknown, but it is possible that they concerned regret over a decision the "Boy General" had made before riding out on his last campaign. As the 7th Cavalry prepared for action, Custer decided to leave behind a battery of Gatling guns because he felt they would slow down his column. The Gatling guns, forerunners of today's machine guns and still in use today in modified form as anti-aircraft weapons, featured multiple barrels arranged in a circle. The circle of barrels was turned by a hand-operated crank, and each discharged in turn, sending forth a deadly spray of bullets. Whether having Gatling guns would have saved Custer is impossible to tell, but one can imagine "Longhair," surrounded by dead troopers and apparently every Indian between St. Louis and the Rocky Mountains, wishing he had the opportunity to find out.

seeking a crossing site, either to support Reno or to hit the camp from the opposite side. At 3:20 P.M., he sent back a trumpeter with an order for Benteen to join him and to bring up the pack train with its reserve ammunition. But Benteen, having come upon Reno's shattered command, decided that he did not have enough strength to support Custer; instead, he had his men dig in alongside Reno's shaken troops. Custer would have to rely on his fabled luck to pull him out.

For once, though, Custer's aggressiveness and vainglory had put him in a predicament from which no amount of luck could rescue him. Moving north against increasing opposition, Custer at some point abandoned any attempt to cross the Little Big Horn and instead sought a defensible position among the gullies and rocky bluffs on the eastern side of the river. He probably hoped to hold out long enough for Benteen's column to relieve him, unaware that no such help was on its way. As increasing numbers of warriors emerged from the village, Custer and his soldiers were forced farther north, until he finally deployed them in a rough V, with himself at the apex.

The Sioux and Cheyenne warriors circled the beleaguered U.S. soldiers warily, crawling forward along the numerous gullies, then popping up to fire on the cavalrymen along the perimeter. Most of those braves who had attacked Reno earlier now joined the fight against Custer. By 5:00 P.M., about 1,600 warriors had Custer's 200 survivors surrounded. The troopers shot their mounts in order to use the corpses as makeshift ramparts, collected ammunition from the dead and wounded, and looked in vain for the arrival of Benteen's men. Their commander watched as each of the five companies succumbed in turn—the little knots of men worn down by arrows and rifle fire, then overwhelmed by a sudden rush of hacking, flailing Native American warriors. Within a quarter of an hour, Custer must have realized there would be no relief, at least not in time. His command reduced to the small band of men around him, Custer, a pistol in each hand, made his last stand. "Longhair [Custer's nickname among the Indians] stood like a sheaf of corn with all the ears fallen around him," an Indian witness recalled. "He killed a man when he fell. He laughed. He had fired his last shot."

Miles away, a patrol from Benteen's battalion saw a swirling dust cloud over the site of the firefight. Gunfire could be heard, faintly, rising to a crescendo and then fading to a few isolated rattles. At 5:25 P.M., the sound of musketry ended altogether, and the patrol turned sadly away to rejoin the remnants of the 7th Cavalry.

Beginning virtually the morning after, debate has raged over who bore the blame for the massacre of Custer's 212 men. Reno and Benteen received a great deal of criticism for failing to support their commander, but it is doubtful whether they could have done more than sacrifice the remainder of the regiment in an effort to cut their way through. It was Custer who discounted the warnings of his scouts, divided his command when his forces were outnumbered three-to-one, and led his battalion into a trap on broken ground that he knew was unsuitable for cavalry. Custer's thirst for glory clouded his judgment and caused the destruction of his regiment. Ironically, because of these blunders, he gained through defeat and death the very glory that he had wanted to attain through victory.

♦ ♦ ♦

Three years after Custer's demise, on ground remarkably similar to the Montana badlands, another colonial army met its unfortunate fate. This time the force defeated was a British regiment operating in southern Africa, but the causes of the disaster were depressingly similar: hubris mixed with carelessness in facing a determined, skillful, and numerous enemy.

In 1879 the British determined to conquer Zululand (part of present-day South Africa) and make it part of the British empire. The powerful Zulu army, under its chief, Cetshwayo, was simply too great a threat to British sovereignty in southern Africa to ignore. In early January, three widely separated columns crossed into Zululand under Lord Chelmsford to search for the Zulu army, which Chelmsford confidently expected his forces to destroy as soon as he could come to grips with it. On January 22, Chelmsford found his quarry—or, rather, it found him.

Above: Custer hard at work in his office at Fort Lincoln, Dakota Territory, three years before his death at Little Big Horn. Top: This depiction of Custer's Land Stand is rife with inaccuracies. Custer, seen here firing two pistols, actually was wearing a buckskin jacket and had cut his long hair short. And in the last stages of the fight, the Indians attacked on foot.

Isandhlwana

We have certainly been seriously underestimating the power of the Zulu army.

—Lord Chelmsford, after the battle

At Isandhlwana, the Zulus launched a classic double envelopment against the overextended British lines.

The bugle call roused the men from their breakfasts, sending them scrambling into formation outside their neat rows of white tents. Within a few moments, the red-coated soldiers of the 1st and 2nd Battalions, 24th Infantry Regiment, stood at attention in the African morning, beneath the beetling brow of the hill known by natives as Isandhlwana. Behind them were five companies of African troops belonging to the 3rd Regiment, Natal Native Contingent (NNC), with their white officers, and a battery of Royal Artillery. The camp commander, Brevet Lieutenant Colonel Henry Burmester Pulleine, emerged from the officer's mess tent, his breakfast uneaten, to see what all the fuss was about.

fighting with bayonets or clubbed rifles amid multitudes of maddened Zulus.

Pulleine saw the end coming. Calmly he rode to the battalion's guard tent, secured the Queen's colors, and ordered his adjutant to try and escape with them. As the young officer rode off, the commander entered his own tent and sat down to pen a farewell note to his wife. The Zulus found him there. Durnford and his loyal horsemen died near the southern end of camp, fighting to the end to hold the way open for those who were able to escape. The Zulus resorted to flinging their own dead onto the horsemen's bayonets before they overwhelmed the men from Natal. Probably the last European to die on the battlefield was Captain Reginald Younghusband, whose company had been bypassed in the initial rush and had sought refuge on higher ground. Younghusband shook hands with each of his men during a lull, then turned to face the Zulu hordes clambering up the slopes toward him. When only the captain and three of his men

The Quartermaster's Blunder

How is it that the British and native soldiers at Isandhlwana ran short of ammunition when more than 500,000 rounds sat in wagons in camp? The answers to that question prove once again that in war the smallest oversights or mistakes can have great consequences.

First of all, the ammunition was packed in separate boxes inside crates secured by nine large screws. Once these screws were removed and the lid taken off the crates, the boxes inside had to be opened. Each box was held shut with six screws, many of which were rusty and therefore hard to start. Each battalion had only one screwdriver, though more were on order (an excuse familiar to many old soldiers). Since you can't unscrew anything with a requisition form, simply getting access to the ammunition was a problem.

The positioning of the ammunition wagons was also a factor. The wagons carrying ammunition for Pulleine's forces were as much as a mile (1.6km) away from the firing line. Durnford's wagons pulled in to camp after the battle began, but no one even knew where they were located.

Compounding all this was the character of the two battalion quartermasters, James Pullen and Edward Bloomfield. Neither man would issue ammunition to anyone outside their battalion—they would turn away haughtily from those who appeared at the wrong wagon. They were also fussily correct in counting out cartridges; every single round had to be accounted for. When desperate soldiers began to hack at the copperbound crates later in the day with axes, bay-onets, and bare hands, the horrified quartermasters tried to stop them until they were driven back with snarled threats of violence.

In defense of Pullen and Bloomfield, it must be said that the two were not mere uniformed bureaucrats. They were also brave men; both died on their feet, defending their precious wagons to the end.

were left, they scrambled onto a wagon, where they held out for some time. At the end, Younghusband alone remained, his tunic gone, swinging his rifle like a madman to hold the respectful Zulus at bay. Finally, he was shot down when one of the Africans brought up a captured gun.

Perhaps 400 men escaped the battlefield, including about 50 Europeans, though not a single man of the 24th survived. Altogether, some 1,400 British soldiers, colonial volunteers, and native levies died at Isandhlwana or were hunted down by pursuing Zulus as they fled. It was the worst defeat the British ever suffered at the hands of a native army. Unfortunately, the man most responsible for the disaster was not present. Lord Chelmsford's arrogant contempt for Cetshwayo's army had led him to divide his expedition in three and then leave the camp at Isandhlwana virtually unprotected. If Pulleine subsequently compounded Chelmsford's blunders with mistakes of his own, at

least he paid full measure for them by dying honorably alongside his men.

Effective resistance to European imperialism stemmed from many sources: fierce loyalty to a favored leader, long traditions of independence, religious zealotry, or simple xenophobia. Few native states exhibited more than two of these traits; only one possessed all four. Ethiopia had defended itself successfully over two millenia against Egyptian, Nubian, Roman, and Arab invaders, inspiring a deep aversion to foreigners. Its royal family, the Emperor Menelik and the Empress Taito, could rely on the absolute loyalty of the Ethiopian peasantry, if not on that of some of the more obstreperous clan chiefs. Most importantly, Ethiopians were united by a deep Christian belief, strengthened by centuries of isolation from other Christian lands and constant fighting with Muslim or animist neighbors.

Several other factors also helped make Ethiopia a very tough nut to crack. Its highlands made up some of the most inhospitable terrain in Africa. Its jagged peaks and jumbled valleys, covered in many places with dense brush, bred tough warriors and provided excellent defensive positions. The few ragged tracks were insufficient to sustain a modern European army, making a prolonged campaign very difficult. And Menelik was canny enough to buy modern rifles, French artillery, and even machine guns for his army. Thus, when Italy invaded in 1895, bent on adding Ethiopia to its colonial empire, it faced a foe that was both numerous and well armed.

Although Lord Chelmsford (inset) was relieved of command after news of the defeat at Isandhlwana (above) reached England, he managed to defeat the Zulus before his replacement arrived.

Adowa

Enemies have come who would ruin our country and change our religion.... With God's help I will get rid of them.

—From Emperor

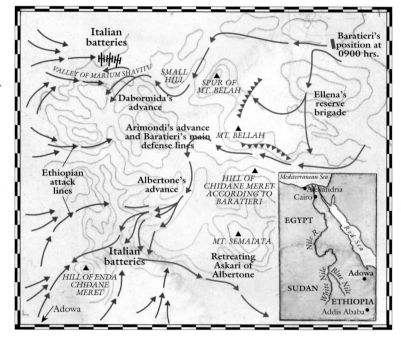

On the evening of February 28, 1896, Italian general Oreste Baratieri presented his four brigade commanders with a difficult choice. After marching into northern Ethiopia, Baratieri's force of 20,000 had spent more than a month in the Tigrean Mountains stymied by Menelik's army, which was ensconced around the town of Adowa. Like wary boxers, the two armies had jabbed at each other, each too respectful of the other's strength to close. Now, though, pressed by his government and painfully aware that his rations were nearly depleted, Baratieri knew that continued inaction was impossible. So he asked his subordinates—should the Italian army attack or retreat?

Unanimously, the brigade leaders counseled attack. Even an unsuccessful assault would serve Italian honor better than ignominious with-

drawal. Baratieri, who had hoped that they would respond this way, proceeded to outline his plan. Under cover of darkness, his four brigades would move up to the line of hills rising above Adowa.

Menelik would then be forced either to attack the Italians in the fortifications they would build there or to withdraw altogether from the town. The first option would certainly spell defeat for the Ethiopians, while the second would show his fractious tribesmen that he had lost his nerve. In either case, the Ethiopian Emperor would be weakened and with him the cause of Ethiopian independence.

Using a sketch map of the surrounding area, Baratieri indicated the positions he wanted each brigade to take. Giuseppe Arimondi's brigade would occupy the center on Mount Belah. Vittorio Dabormida's brigade would be on his right, with a third brigade in reserve on the backside of Mount Belah. Baratieri then moved his finger across the map to indicate the position the left flank should take—an inconspicuous knob known as Chidane Meret, which was to be defended by the *Askaris*, native infantrymen under Brigadier General Matteo Albertone. With this, the first link in the chain of disaster was formed.

Above: Local guides took Albertone's brigade to the hill of Enda Chirane Meret, which was mismarked on the Italian maps, and thereby unhinged the entire Italian defense. Top: While many Western generals lost battles with native armies, General Oreste Baratieri was among the few to lose a war. Right: An engraving of Ethopia's Emperor Menelik, mounted on horseback and armed with a modern repeating rifle.

Around 9:00 P.M. on the moonless night of February 29 (1896 was a leap year), the Italians moved out through the twisting, narrow canyons. Local guides led each of the brigades to their positions, where cursing *bersaglieri* (the infamous Italian mountain infantry) and Askari began to dig in. News of the Italian advance reached the Ethiopian emperor as he kneeled in morning prayer. Menelik at first disbelieved the reports, but subsequently declared that God had delivered his people. The Ethiopians, suffering even greater privations than the Italians, were already preparing to abandon Adowa, a move scheduled for the second day of March. Instead, Menelik now had the opportunity to meet the Italians away from their prepared positions. He ordered his warriors to prepare for battle.

As the sun rose on March 1, Baratieri puzzled over the location of Albertone's brigade. He could plainly see the hill marked on his map as Chidane Meret, but there was no sign of Albertone. Assuming that the brigadier had moved slightly forward of the hill, Baratieri dispatched runners to

direct Albertone to the correct location, then turned his attention to the remainder of his army. Meanwhile, Albertone was similarly confused. His native guides affirmed that his men were digging in on Chidane Meret, but his right-hand units could find no sign of Arimondi's brigade, which should have been just off their flank.

In fact, Albertone was 3 miles (4.8km) forward of his assigned position. The Italian sketch map had Chidane Meret marked incorrectly, and the locals guiding the Italian column, who did not use maps, brought Albertone exactly where he had told them he wanted to go. As a result, Albertone's Askaris were dangerously exposed, while Baratieri's left flank was wide open.

The brigadier had little time to work out what had happened, for he was soon under attack from three sides by Menelik's aroused warriors. Though partially armed with modern weapons, the Ethiopians still fought in undisciplined masses, rushing forward piecemeal to close with the enemy. Cooperation between clans was nonexistent, allowing Albertone's men to repulse one attack

after another. But the rocky valleys continued to disgorge endless streams of warriors. Baratieri had assured his generals that the Ethiopian emperor had at most 30,000 tribesmen—estimates of 60,000 were dismissed as wild fantasy. By midmorning, the larger number no longer seemed so fantastic.

The truth was even worse than the most pessimistic Italian might have imagined, for Menelik had mustered close to 100,000 warriors around Adowa. Almost half of these, whipped to a frenzy by the Empress Taito, who brazenly exposed herself to enemy fire, were unleashed against Albertone. With Taito's encouragements ringing in their ears, 50,000 screaming warriors finally overran the Askari entrenchments and poured down the valley toward Baratieri.

Above: The city of Adowa in 1896. Opposite: A European sketch of the Ethiopian army on the march to Adowa. Inset: The Emperor Menelik a few years after the battle. He not only defied the colonial powers of Europe, but also expanded the Ethiopian state at the expense of his neighbors.

General Baratieri, under the impression for most of the morning that Albertone was only slightly forward, had responded to the brigadier's pleas for reinforcements by sending up Dabormida's brigade. Dabormida was told to make contact with Albertone and help him to pull back to his proper position on the Italian left. Unfortunately, the Italians again fell victim to their unfamiliarity with the area. Since one canyon looked much like another, Dabormida turned the wrong way, blundering off to the right. Just about the time that Albertone's brigade was going under, Dabormida stumbled upon the left wing of Menelik's army, which he promptly waded into, convinced that his beleaguered colleague must be just ahead.

Baratieri, meantime, was growing increasingly muddled. Two of his brigades had seemingly disappeared into thin air, though the sound of rifle and cannon fire echoed through the hills. For an hour or more he failed to take any real action, instead sending orders or requests for information to Albertone (who was dead) and to Dabormida (who was by now cut off). If he had gathered his remaining men and gone forward, or cut his losses and

beat a hasty retreat, defeat would not have turned into catastrophe. In an agony of indecision, he did neither.

At about 10:30 A.M., refugees from Albertone's shattered formation began to appear in front of Baratieri, closely followed by thousands of Ethiopians. The wave crashed against Arimondi's Alpine troops, who held on desperately for an hour, their artillery tearing gaping wounds in the closely packed masses of tribesmen. But, outnumbered ten to one, the Italian forces could not resist for long, and once Baratieri sounded the retreat the entire Italian line disintegrated in a rout.

The only bright spot for the Italians was the conduct of Dabormida's brigade. As perplexed as any other Italian general on that day, Dabormida was not even aware he was surrounded until two hours after the center had fallen apart. The brigadier finally determined to cut his way out of the trap, and led his men in a brilliant, though costly, fighting retreat. They were the only Italian units to emerge in good order from the battle, though their general did not survive to see it. His body was found months later among his fallen men.

Baratieri had led some 17,000 men forward to Adowa on that last night of

February 1896. The next day, after a defeat that was largely the result of faulty maps and navigational errors (that is, losing their way), only 9,200 shocked survivors, nearly 1,500 of them wounded, emerged from the battle. Although Menelik's army had also suffered dearly, the Italians withdrew permanently from Ethiopia, the only African nation to preserve its independence up to the First World War.

✦ ✦ ✦

If one considers only this Italian defeat and the other Western losses that preceded it, it may seem that empire builders were the only blunderers of the colonial period. Actually, Westerners held no monopoly on military incompetence. At Little Big Horn, Isandhlwana, and Adowa, native leaders displayed tactical finesse and a keen appreciation for terrain; at Omdurman, where the Muslim Khalifa of Sudan tried to turn back an Anglo-Egyptian invasion, none of these qualities were in evidence. The Khalifa and his generals, blunderers of the highest order, relied on the zeal of their Dervishes to bring victory, but they discovered that bravery was no match for the machine gun and the magazine-fed rifle.

Omdurman

Cease fire! Please! Cease fire. What a dreadful waste of ammunition!

—Lord Kitchener

The morning of September 2, 1898, dawned cool, but with the promise of suffocating desert heat to follow. On the bank of the Nile just below the Sudanese capitol of Omdurman, 25,000 English and Egyptian troops under Major General Horatio Herbert Kitchener anxiously watched for signs of activity among the Sudanese. Kitchener feared that the 50,000-man army of the Khalifa, Sudan's military, religious, and political leader, might stay within the walls of Omdurman or slip away to the south. Staying in Omdurman would result in costly and protracted street fighting; slipping away to the south would mean an expensive guerrilla war. What Kitchener wanted was a pitched battle to end a campaign that had already dragged on for two and a half years. The British commander, who in the convoluted manner of imperial politics was also commander, or *Sirdar*, of the Egyptian army, did not have to wait long to discover the Khalifa's intentions. An hour after dawn, the Sudanese army emerged to do battle.

It was an impressive sight, one that has not been repeated since. Clustered behind their immense banners, clothed in white battle dress, some wearing chain mail, the Khalifa's army crested the low hills that ringed Kitchener's

The Khalifa's army hurled itself piecemeal against forces led by Lord Kitchener (above left), which were comfortably ensconced with both flanks on the Nile.

position. They came on in a crescent 4 miles (6.4km) wide, spears or rifles in one hand, Korans in the other, and battle cries rising into the desert air. To the watching Anglo-Egyptian army, some 2 miles (3.2km) distant across a featureless plain, the chanting sounded like the angry droning of hornets.

Kitchener's men had their backs to the Nile, so there was no danger to their flanks. Forty-four modern artillery pieces and a dozen Maxim machine guns were scattered along the front. Six gunboats offered further support from the river. The British regulars had Lee-Metford repeating rifles, and they had filed the tips off their ammunition, making the .303-caliber rounds into improvised dumdum bullets (which expand more than usual upon striking their target, thus causing greater damage). The Egyptian troops carried the older (but reliable) Martini-Henry breechloaders. In all, Kitchener possessed a terrific advantage in firepower, and the Khalifa was sending his soldiers into the perfect killing field, devoid of cover or concealment. It was exactly the sort of engagement Kitchener hoped for.

For reasons never properly explained, most of the 50,000 Dervishes pulled up just out of range, leaving only about 14,000 to charge the British lines at a steady trot. The artillery was the first weaponry employed against this mass, followed by the machine guns. When the Sudanese came within 2,000 yards (1,820m) the British initiated volley fire in the old style, the front rank kneeling and the rear rank firing over their heads. At 800

Map labels:

Mediterranean Sea
Alexandria
Cairo
EGYPT
Nile R.
Red Sea
Omdurman
Khartoum
SUDAN
White Nile
Blue Nile
ETHIOPIA
Addis Ababa

HILLS OF KARERI
ABU ZERIBA
DAHAM

Army of Green Flag (4,000 men)

Sheik of Din (10,000 men in reserve)

Osman Azrak (8,000 men)

British defensive lines

Kitchener (25,000 men, 44 guns)

Farthest limit of Mahdist attack

JEBEL SURGHAM

Army of Black Flag (12,000 men)

Khalifa's HQ (1,000 men)

Kara Army (4,000 men)

Charge of 21st Lancers

Khur Abu Sunt

Nile River

Omdurman

Osman Digna (700 men in ambush)

Above: Perversely, the most celebrated incident of Omdurman is the pointless charge of the 21st Lancers into a gully aswarm with the enemy. In the years following this debacle, numerous artists created paintings depicting the moment the British cavalry stumbled upon the hidden Sudanese. The above painting is by Stanley Berkeley; the one on pages 88–89 is by Richard Caton Woodville. Below: A fanciful period engraving of the Dervish attack. In reality, the Sudanese never got this close.

yards (728m), the Egyptians joined in the carnage. For an hour the Dervishes came on, but not one man reached the Anglo-Egyptian lines. One group managed to reach a sandy ridge about 300 yards (273m) distant, and from there they picked off a few defenders before being torn apart by shrapnel—but that was it. By 8:30 A.M., the firing ended; the attackers had fled, leaving behind 2,000 mangled corpses and hundreds more men wounded too badly to crawl away. Only a handful of Kitchener's men had fallen.

For the moment, the battle appeared to be over. Some Dervishes continued to skirmish, taking potshots at the British as they formed up to march on the city, but otherwise the field remained quiet. Now, in his eagerness to seize Omdurman, Kitchener almost lost the battle that had begun so promisingly.

After the Anglo-Egyptian army sorted itself out and began its trek along the Nile, the rear brigade was inadvertently left a mile (1.6km) or more behind. The greater part of the Khalifa's army, unengaged so far, now reappeared to swoop down on the four native battalions commanded by a lantern-jawed Scot brigadier named Hector MacDonald. Luckily for Kitchener, the Sudanese leader failed to

Young Winston

The casualty count at Omdurman would have been even more lopsided had it not been for the blunder of one Lieutenant Colonel Rowland Hill Martin, commander of the 21st Lancers. This regiment, through no fault of its own, was the only regular cavalry outfit in the British Army without a battle honor inscribed on its colors. The officers and men had for years suffered the jibe that their motto was "Thou Shalt Not Kill," and they were eager to prove themselves in combat. Their impatience during the first phase at Omdurman, when Kitchener's infantry and artillery were doing their butcher's work, was manifest. By the time the fidgeting troopers were ordered to reconnoiter the route into Omdurman, the slaughter appeared to be over, and Martin was wild to do something—anything—to prove his men's mettle.

As the Lancers cantered out from behind the sheltering arms of the infantry, Martin spotted a few stray Sudanese off to the left. Instead of driving them off with a few volleys from the carbines that every Lancer carried, Martin decided to launch a full-scale regimental charge over unfamiliar ground. One of the participants in this charge was the young Winston Churchill (the future prime minister of England), who has left an extraordinary account of the event. As the 21st broke into a gallop, lances lowered, the Sudanese valiantly turned and fired, spurning safety in an attempt to kill a few infidels. The Lancers bowled them over easily, but just beyond them the plain suddenly fell away into a gully, which was invisible until the last moment. Concealed in the gully were 2,000 Sudanese warriors. Unable to check their momentum, the 400 men of the 21st plunged into the rabid mass. For two minutes, as the regiment rode through to the far side of the gully, turned, and cut their way back, a pandemonium of shots, screams, and the clash of steel ensued. Had the Sudanese not been as surprised as the British, few of the Lancers would have escaped. As it was, 70 lancers were killed or wounded, and another 50 or so unhorsed. In other words, 16 percent of Kitchener's casualties at Omdurman resulted from a completely unnecessary (not to mention worthless) cavalry charge. Lieutenant Colonel Martin, nevertheless, was pleased, for his regiment had at last won its spurs.

❖ ❖ ❖

For the native peoples of the world, the tragedy of colonial warfare arose out of the bitter truth that not even victory could avert the ultimate triumph of the modern states. Within a decade after Custer's defeat (indeed, partly because of it), the power of the Plains Indians was permanently broken; Cetshwayo's Zulus never again defeated the British army, and in fact were overwhelmed before the year was out; the Italians would return to Ethiopia in the 1930s, but this time with planes, tanks, and poison gas, weapons a new generation of warriors could not overcome.

The Little Wars (the term for the colonial wars of the late nineteenth century) also exerted a baleful influence on European armies. Diverted by their colonial adventures, European states did not make war on each other for decades. Between 1855 and the beginning of World War I in 1914, Great Britain fought against no other major power; similarly, France and Germany remained at peace from 1871 until 1914; and the last major conflicts of Austria-Hungary or Italy before the Great War took place in 1866. Thus, there arose two generations of European soldiers whose only combat experience came in brushfire wars against relatively primitive forces. As a result, these armies perfected the offensive use of technologically advanced weapons (in particular, the machine gun and powerful modern artillery) without ever learning how to defend themselves against them. Furthermore, officers learned tactics and absorbed attitudes that served them well against unsophisticated enemies but had absolutely no place on a European battlefield.

In essence, the military lessons learned in the years of colonial wars were largely inapplicable to modern warfare. Science and technology had raced ahead of Europe's warriors, creating weapons that these soldiers and tacticians did not know how to overcome. Consequently, World War I, the next great conflict between European forces, became the worst bloodbath the world had ever known.

5

ST. PRIVAT • SPION KOP
THE WESTERN FRONT

Total War

The era of mass warfare slowly gave way to the age of total war, a type of warfare that engaged not just a nation's manpower, but also its industry, agriculture, science, and technology—the state's entire resources. Modern farms and factories, linked by a highly developed road and rail network, could support huge armies in the field almost indefinitely. Technological advances in metallurgy, chemistry, and weapons design equipped legions with arms of previously unimaginable destructive capability. Together, these changes necessitated an entirely new style of military leadership.

Elements of this change in the nature of war had been discernible during the American Civil War, but it was not until World War I that the shattering reality of total war was revealed. During the five decades between these two conflicts, Europe and the United States enjoyed a time of relative peace and great prosperity. The few major wars of this era offered glimpses of the battlefields of the future and were intently studied by warriors of all nations, but only a handful of tacticians correctly foresaw what these wars portended. As a result, when Europe again went to war in 1914, commanders were faced with tactical and strategic problems that they were unprepared to solve. In truth, some of these problems were insoluble: The effectiveness of the defender, strongly dug into trenches bristling with machine guns and powerful artillery, had advanced so far that all but the most limited attacks were doomed to costly failure. Wiser heads realized this, but too often they did not prevail against those who developed one faulty scheme after another for breaking the enemy's trench line.

The only major European conflict between 1866 and 1914 was the Franco-Prussian War. This war was largely the result of the competition for continental dominance between a rapidly expanding Prussia and a declining French Empire ruled by Napoleon Bonaparte's namesake and nephew, Napoleon III. The Prussian army, organized with Teutonic efficiency by its brilliant chief of staff, Helmuth von Moltke, ran roughshod over Napoleon III's forces. By August 1870, a scant month after the outbreak of hostilities, most of the French Army was nearly cut off around the fortress of Metz. On August 18, Moltke's armies cut the last few escape routes leading north from Metz. The French, under Marshal François Achille Bazaine, struggled to keep them open, bringing on the battle of Gravelotte-St. Privat. The whys and wherefores of this campaign do not interest us so much as one incident from the battle that foreshadowed the slaughter that would occur during World War I.

Opposite: The face of total war. A soldier and his horse sport gas masks on the western front during World War I.

St. Privat

I have given up asking after friends as I get to each question no other answer than 'dead' or 'wounded.'

—Julius von Verdy du Vernois, Prussian staff officer

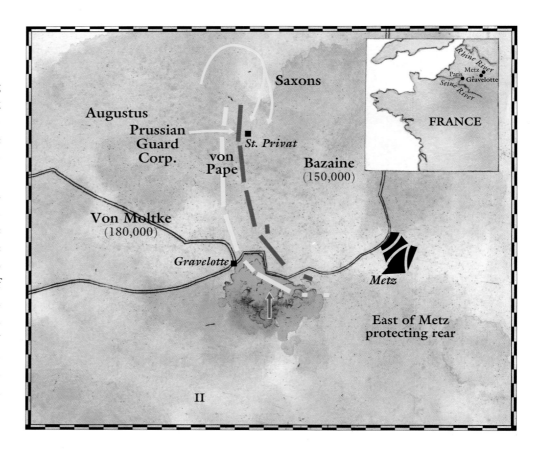

Above: St. Privat guarded the last remaining escape route for the French around Metz. Top: Napoleon III shared his famous uncle's ambition and political flair, but inherited little of his military genius.

Prince Augustus of Württemberg twisted in the saddle to check the sun's position. It hovered, smoke-dimmed, a hand's breadth above the horizon. Perhaps three hours of daylight remained on August 18, 1870. Only three hours, the last of which would be rapidly fading twilight. Opposite Augustus's Guard Corps, the elite formation of Prussia's army, the French clung grimly to the little hilltop village of St. Privat, the right anchor of their line. The 180 Prussian cannon had already pounded their French counterparts to bits, but the enemy infantry remained entrenched on the bare slopes below the hamlet. Augustus was determined that St. Privat would be in his hands before night fell.

To that end, two divisions of the Royal Saxon Corps had swung north and then eastward to envelop the French right. The Guard Corps' orders were to pin down the French forces while the Saxons descended on their flank. If the maneuver proved successful, the French army's escape routes to the north would be cut off, and they would have to fall back into the fortress at Metz. Once that occurred, half of Napoleon III's troops would be trapped inside. But the Saxons seemed to be taking an inordinately long time getting into position, and Augustus feared they might come too late. His superior, the Prussian prince Frederick Charles, commander of Prussia's Second Army, agreed. Frederick Charles, impetuous at the best of times, authorized Augustus to attack the French positions straightaway.

Augustus hurriedly passed the order on to his division commanders. General von Pape, commander of the 1st Guards Division, protested strongly that a frontal assault had little chance for success. He begged that he at least be allowed to have the Prussian artillery plaster the French positions before his men went forward. The stern Augustus cut him short, peremptorily directing him to get on with it. Both officers proudly displayed an impressive set of mustachios: Augustus's were as wide as his ears and waxed to fine points, while von Pape's curved downward to blend in with sideburns that cascaded from ear to chin. The two now bristled at each other for a long, electric moment, until von Pape angrily saluted and stalked away.

At 6:00 P.M., the 30,000 men of the Guard Corps deployed for the attack. A thick skirmish line moved out ahead of the main body; the remainder stood to in company columns, awaiting the signal to advance. Although the Guard Corps might not have been the best infantry in Europe, it was certainly the most aristocratic. Scions of Germany's royal families fought to enter its ranks, and few officers who served in this corps did not have the noble *von* preceding their names.

Bugle calls and drumbeats heralded the opening of the attack. The skirmish line trotted briskly forward; behind it, four brigades marched toward St. Privat, a mile (1.6km) away up gently sloping fields. The Prussians had been trained to advance in company-size formations while taking advantage of folds in the terrain to shield them from the enemy, but the hillside before them rose so uniformly that virtually every square yard (0.84 sq m) was exposed. On the high ground, French soldiers adjusted the sights on their excellent chassepot rifles, which were accurate to a distance of 800 yards (728m) and capable of hitting massed formations at double that range.

Before long, French rifle fire began to snap overhead—troops firing downhill often overestimate the distance to their targets—and then the rounds began to strike home with devastating effectiveness. Within minutes every mounted officer was down. Captains and lieutenants urged their units on, and the soldiers of the Guard Corps responded magnificently, trudging forward hunched over like men advancing into a rainstorm. As more and more

Frenchmen found the range, the sound of slugs hitting bodies made a steady muffled patter. Entire companies melted away, heaped up like cordwood where the fire was hottest, leaving a trail of dead and wounded where the rifle fire was relatively less deadly.

Formations began to break up as men fell and survivors instinctively picked up the pace. The attack decayed into a single dark blue wave, impelled by aristocratic honor, bugle calls, and the shouts of the few surviving officers. Implacably, the French continued to fire methodically into the Prussian ranks, until even the hardiest guardsmen began seeking refuge against the bare earth. Before long, the advance petered out. A few determined groups of men rushed forward in short bounds

Below left: Prince Augustus of Württemberg's impatience resulted in the death or wounding of over a quarter of his corps in less than half an hour. Below right: General Von Pape, commander of the 1st Guards Division, foresaw the slaughter of his men, but carried out his order in fine Prussian tradition.

or crawled on their bellies, but most simply clutched the ground. Six hundred yards (546m) from St. Privat, the Guard Corps halted of its own accord, the shaken soldiers unwilling either to resume the advance or to flee back across the killing ground.

In twenty minutes, 8,000 guardsmen had been killed or wounded. For another hour, the remnants of the corps lay motionless in front of St. Privat, their only salvation coming in the form of covering fire from their artillery batteries, which had been belatedly brought into action. Finally, the dilatory Saxons, descending as planned from the north, easily squeezed the remaining Frenchmen out of St. Privat, ending the ordeal of the Prussian soldiers pinned down on the naked slopes below the village.

What distinguishes the brutal sacrifice of infantry at St. Privat from similar dreary examples, such as Pickett's Charge at Gettysburg seven years earlier, is that the carnage was wrought without the aid of artillery. Nine battalions of French infantry at St. Privat had worked as much destruction as two Union corps and more than a hundred

The Saxons storm St. Privat from the north after the destruction of the Guards. Ironically, the French commander at St. Privat, General Canrobert, had witnessed the Charge of the Light Brigade sixteen years before.

The Wonder Weapon

Napoleon III, though something of a bungler on the battlefield, was a great weapons enthusiast and quite a tinkerer. In 1866 under his guidance, the French Army came up with the *mitrailleuse*, a carriage-mounted weapon that boasted 25 concentrically arranged barrels capable of accurately delivering 125 rounds a minute at a range of up to 2,700 yards (2,457m). Unfortunately for the French, Napoleon III was petrified at the thought that the Prussians might steal his design, so the mitrailleuse was locked up under great secrecy.

Issued only days before the war began, the mitrailleuse was unfamiliar to its crews and their commanders. Having never had the opportunity to train with it, French officers tended to ignore it or deploy it improperly, in either case wasting the great advantage it might have given them. The crews, lacking more than rudimentary practice in firing or maintaining this weapon, rarely got the most out of its tremendous potential. On those rare occasions when the weapons were handled well and properly emplaced, the Prussians treated them with great respect, making Napoleon III's mitrailleuse one of history's great might-have-beens.

---

cannon at Gettysburg. The spectacular increase in killing power brought about by the advent of the breech-loading rifle was making frontal assaults against entrenched infantry a near-suicidal endeavor. The Prussians, for the most part, learned this lesson, and few repeated Prince Augustus's blunder—at least not until the next war.

✦ ✦ ✦

In 1899, about thirty years after the Prussian defeat at St. Privat, the British army received its first taste of total war. Just beyond the British Cape Colony in southern Africa lay the independent Boer republics of the Transvaal and the Orange Free State. The Boers, or Afrikaaners, were descendants of Dutch colonists who had fled British encroachments for the vast interior of Africa. These white men had lived in Africa for so many generations that they considered themselves as "native" as the Africans they so brutally exploited. Unfortunately, the land they tilled covered large gold deposits, a source of wealth coveted by the rapacious Europeans. Rather than lose this treasure to one of their colonial rivals, England provoked a war with the Boers.

The British expected an easy campaign, but they were soon disillusioned. The hardy Boers, every one of whom was a crackerjack rider, quickly carried the war to British colonial soil, surrounding various outposts in the Cape Colony and the province of Natal. When relief columns approached the beleaguered British garrisons, the Boers used their repeating rifles and a handful of modern artillery pieces (supplied by a sympathetic Germany) to inflict stunning defeats on the overconfident British. As 1899 passed into 1900, the British made one more attempt to reach the besieged city of Ladysmith in Natal. To do so, they had to pass a range of hills between them and the town. In January 1900, they attempted to seize the highest of these peaks.

Spion Kop

If your men had our generals, where should we Boers be?

—Captured Boer officer

The South African night, dimly lit by a quarter moon and blanketed by thin mist, cloaked the approach of Lieutenant Colonel A.W. Thorneycroft's Mounted Infantry to the peak of Spion Kop. The men had left their mounts behind, as well as their spurs, which the soldiers feared might clink on the rocky hillside and warn the enemy of their approach. Magazines were also deliberately empty, lest an accidental discharge give them away to the Boers holding the summit. Just above Thorneycroft's men, muttered conversations revealed the presence of sentries. Thorneycroft motioned for the battalion to deploy, and the men noiselessly spread out into a thin line. Bayonets clicked softly into place, as the whispered command "Creep forward" was passed down the formation. On hands and knees, the infantry edged closer.

With Ladysmith under siege, the British in Natal attempted to break through the Boer lines. It was believed that taking Spion Kop would force the Boers to retreat.

From behind them, the noise of some bumbler dropping his pick alerted the Boers. "*Wie's daar?*" challenged the nearest sentry. For a moment, every man on the summit, Boer and Briton, froze in place. Then the silence was shattered by Mauser rifles blazing away from the Boer outpost. Thorneycroft's dragoons threw themselves flat, in accordance with their carefully planned attack, until they could hear the bolts clicking on empty chambers. As the Boers fumbled to reload, the battalion rose as one and charged with their bayonets. The Boer pickets fled, as did the hundred or so sleeping men behind them, roused by the exchange. Many abandoned their boots and rifles, so great was their haste to escape.

Thorneycroft had good reason to feel well satisfied with the operation. At a cost of only three wounded, he had secured Spion Kop. On the morrow, the whole range of hills blocking the advance to Ladysmith would fall under the domination of British guns. As a prearranged signal that Spion Kop had fallen, Thorneycroft had his men belt out three cheers. It was an auspicious beginning for a bloody debacle.

By now it was nearly dawn, and reinforcements followed the men of the Mounted Infantry onto Spion Kop. Two more infantry battalions— the Royal Lancasters and the Lancashire Fusiliers—plus assorted Royal Engineers and signalmen, brought British strength on the summit to a grand total of 1,700. Major General E.R. Woodgate arrived to take command, immediately ordering the troops to begin digging in.

Now things began to go wrong. No one had anticipated that the ground might be too hard to construct entrenchments, but it was. The sweating, cursing soldiers could scratch out no more than a foot or two (30–60cm) before hitting bedrock. Though they supplemented this with stones, most men had little more than a shallow ditch in which to take shelter. Sandbags were an obvious solution, but they had been forgotten. In any case, the soldiers, in the dark, on the unfa-

miliar hilltop, had dug the trench (such as it was) in the wrong location. When morning came, Woodgate saw to his horror that the crest of the hill ran 50 yards (15m), at its closest point, to 200 yards (60m), at its farthest point, in front of his position. This meant that any counterattacking Boer troops could clamber up the backside of Spion Kop unseen until they reached the lip of the summit. Because of this, all advantage of holding the high ground disappeared. Woodgate had no choice but to abandon the trench his troops had labored over for hours and move them out to the crest to start over.

The sun burned away the morning mist to reveal more bad news. Spion Kop might be the highest peak in the area, but several other nearby hilltops were only slightly lower. From these there now came Boer rifle and artillery fire, sweeping Spion Kop with deadly effect. Before they had a chance to dig in, Woodgate's men were driven from the crest back to the dubious cover of their previous entrenchments. This allowed Boer troops to move up to the

crest, as Woodgate had feared, and lash the position with point-blank fire from their Mauser rifles.

The battle quickly assumed a pattern. To drive away their assailants, the British emerged from cover, stormed to the crest, and sent the Boers bounding back down the rock-strewn hillside. This in turn exposed the attackers to renewed artillery fire, which forced them to retire to their shallow trench. Cautiously, the Boers would then creep back up, and the whole wearisome cycle would begin again.

Although the repeated Boer assaults were annoying, they did not lead to many casualties. The biggest killers throughout the day were shrapnel from the artillery and rifle fire from

A glaringly inaccurate picture of the fighting around Spion Kop. The greatest fault is the depiction of the Boers along the far slope—few British soldiers ever saw the wily Boer marksmen who plagued them througout the day.

snipers. As many as ten shells a minute landed on Spion Kop, spraying the crowded summit with metal and stone fragments. The slaughter among the 1,700 men crammed into the 1,600-square-yard (1,280-sq-m) position was indescribable. And Boer marksmen, some firing from as much as 1,500 yards (1,365m) away, sent bullet after bullet into the brains of those incautious enough to expose themselves for more than an instant. Woodgate was struck down by sniper fire early on; in the confusion of battle few on the hilltop knew he was down, and the defenders were left essentially leaderless.

As the survivors huddled miserably behind their makeshift defenses, confused reports were filtering down from the summit to the headquarters of Lieutenant General Sir Charles Warren, the commander responsible for the entire operation. This worthy did little other than order up reinforcements, who could do nothing under the circumstances except offer the Boers fresh targets. Warren should have instead used these reinforcements to attack the Boer-held peaks surrounding Spion Kop. In all likelihood, such attacks would have succeeded, for the Boers were concentrating all their strength against Spion Kop; even if unsuccessful, the pressure on the British would have been relieved enough to evacuate the wounded and bring up fresh supplies of water, medicine, and ammunition.

Warren's inaction can be partly explained by the idiocy of General Talbot Coke, who commanded the troops on and around Spion Kop. Coke positioned himself some distance from the summit, where he intercepted most of the frantic messages coming down from battalion commanders, surrounded by their dead and unable to find Woodgate, whom most believed was still alive. Coke, who visited the top only once, and briefly at that, summarily dismissed the notes as exaggerations, and failed to pass them on. (In one hastily scrawled note, Thorneycroft described the charnel house Spion Kop had become and pleaded for reinforcements, sandbags,

and water. He ended the note by begging Warren to attack the enemy's gun positions. Coke read the message, sent two battalions up to the summit, and reported laconically to Warren, "We appear to be holding our own.")

Night finally brought an end to the long agony of the British troops on Spion Kop. Darkness allowed the surviving commanders to meet in a hollow behind the trench now choked with dead. Once Woodgate's fate had become known, Warren had put Thorneycroft in charge of all troops on the hilltop, but the remaining battalion commanders did not know this until they met with him that evening. Thorneycroft had fought courageously all day long, incredibly escaping with only a sprained ankle, but his nerve was spent after eleven hours of incessant barrage, sniper fire, and Boer assaults. As far as Thorneycroft could tell, Warren planned to leave the British on the hill for another long day of murder, which he knew they could not endure. During the day, large groups had already surrendered, stumbling toward Boer lines under makeshift white flags; they preferred capture by the Boers to waiting on the hill for a bullet or piece of shrapnel to find them. On his own initiative, Thorneycroft abandoned the hill, using the night to cover the retreat of the troops as it had covered their advance that morning. Better to give up the hill, he thought, than to wait and allow the Boers to mop up six battalions the next day.

By midnight, the withdrawal was well under way. Ironically, the Boers were also retreating, discouraged by their failure to dislodge the British from Spion Kop. If Thorneycroft had held his position, the next morning would have marked a British victory—with the Boers gone, the British would have won the day by default. Instead, when the Boers realized that Spion Kop was unoccupied, they jubilantly retook it.

With Spion Kop lost to the Boers, the British retired, leaving Ladysmith to its fate. Of the 4,000 men who fought on Spion Kop over the course of that long day, at least one in four became

casualties: 243 were killed outright, and many more died of their wounds as they slid and bounced down the hill, despite the best efforts of their exhausted stretcher bearers. It is said the Boers wept at the sight when they surveyed the hilltop the morning after Thorneycroft abandoned it.

In many ways, this admittedly minor action gave its participants a taste of the Great War to come. Modern artillery, fired from well beyond rifle range, made occupation of any piece of ground costly unless the troops were securely dug in. The troops involved could not strike back at such an enemy—they could only endure. It was up to their leaders to eliminate the threat somehow, but Warren and Coke could not think of any alternatives; all they could do was feed fresh bodies into the meat grinder. This was a solution that would be applied on a much larger scale in World War I.

By the time the Great War began in 1914, the lessons paid for in blood at a dozen sanguinary battles had partially faded from military consciousness. St. Privat had demonstrated the futility of the frontal attack, Omdurman the power of the machine gun, Spion Kop the lethality of modern artillery, and there were myriad examples of the importance of entrenchments, but somehow all this never quite settled in the minds of most soldiers. There were exceptions, to be sure, but military journals of the time continued to debate most fiercely the design of new cavalry sabers or the best way to instill in soldiers the "spirit of the bayonet."

Military men were no less intelligent in 1914 than in previous times, but the First World War ushered in a completely new style of warfare, and many soldiers could not adjust. Officers who had trained for the dashing cavalry charge, the bayonet assault, and the brilliant maneuver that brought victory could not easily abandon the ingrained attitudes of a lifetime when faced with the utterly alien experience of trench warfare.

The Western Front

Flesh versus iron, concrete, flame, and wire.

—Gilbert Frankau, World War I
German soldier and poet

By the winter of 1914, the western front had congealed. The lines ran uninterruptedly from the English Channel to the border of Switzerland, and though not every stretch was entrenched, both armies were digging away like beavers. Trench systems, backed by dug-in artillery, protected by tangles of barbed wire, and manned by troops employing machine guns, hand grenades, and magazine-fed rifles, zigzagged across the French and Belgian countryside. In some places the lines nearly touched, but mostly there was a fairly extensive no-man's-land separating the Germans from the Allies.

Since it was impossible to outflank the enemy—one end of the line was anchored on the sea and the other on neutral territory—generals on both sides pondered how best to break through the formidable defenses frontally. General Joseph Joffre, chief of the French general staff, was an unquenchable optimist firmly wedded to the belief that the offensive spirit could overcome the stoutest defense. In February 1915, after concentrating what he considered an overwhelming force in Champagne, he hammered at the German lines on a 10-mile (16km) front. Wave after wave of enthusiastic

After the Germans failed to capture Paris in 1914, the trench lines remained static (with only minor shifts) from 1915 through 1917. In 1918 the Germans nearly broke through, but the failure of their final offensive led to their subsequent collapse

poilus (the French nickname for the average infantryman, equivalent to the American "doughboy"), promised that this offensive would end the war, crashed against the German trenches for over a month. They gained 2 miles (3.2km) at their deepest penetration—perhaps a dozen square miles (31.2 sq km) of territory altogether—before the

offensive was called off. To achieve this slight gain, the French suffered more than 240,000 casualties.

Farther north, around the town of Neuve Chapelle, the British conducted their own offensive. The colorless Lieutenant General Sir Douglas Haig, commander of the British First Army, was assigned the task of capturing Aubers Ridge, the high ground that dominated the territory around the city of Lille. The British, observing the failure of Joffre's offensive, decided to initiate their own attack on March 10. They hoped to avoid heavy casualties by precisely mapping out a scheme of maneuvers integrating artillery fire with infantry assaults. They constructed an elaborate timetable, which began with an intensive artillery bombardment that was expected to cut the Germans' barbed wire and smash their trenches. Unfortunately, a shortage of artillery ammunition meant the bombardment would have to be limited to just over half an hour.

As it turned out, the bombardment worked well—too well. The intensity of the barrage hewed paths through the wire and did considerable damage to the entrenchments, and its short duration gave insufficient warning time for the Germans to assemble their reserves.

The two British corps in the attack quickly gained their initial objectives—the resistance was slight—but then dithered about, their meticulously prepared timetable upset, while the Germans formed a new line in front of them. When Haig finally sorted matters out and renewed the attack, his soldiers, bereft of artillery support, died in droves before the enemy's improvised positions. The attack petered out by the third day, though not before the British had lost 11,000 men for 1,000 yards (910m) of churned earth.

Throughout the summer, the Allies pondered the spring battles, obtusely drawing all the wrong conclusions. They believed that the early success at Neuve Chapelle was the result of the violence of the preliminary bombardment, when in fact it was the surprise afforded by a short barrage that allowed the attackers to overwhelm the initial trench line; they attributed the failure of the

Above: These Frenchmen occupy trenches around Verdun. Below: Training for a new kind of war, these soldiers practice hurling grenades from a mock-up trench while wearing gas masks.

French attacks to the late commitment of reserves, when it is doubtful that any mass of men could have forced their way into open country; finally, the British believed that they could use gas as decisively as the

Germans had at Ypres, though by now the Germans were prepared for that weapon also. Assured they had at last found the key to breaking the stalemate, the Allies prepared a massive offensive for September.

The British and French planned to punch through the German lines in two places. The French in the south would repeat their attack in Champagne, while a combined Anglo-French offensive would crack open the line between Loos and Arras. Masses of artillery were concentrated alongside huge stocks of laboriously accumulated ammunition to provide for a prolonged bombardment of unparalleled intensity. Reserves took up positions close behind the first waves. Cavalry divisions assembled further back to exploit the anticipated gaps. Buses were even parked nearby to transport infantry rapidly once the enemy began its headlong retreat. Arrows on staff maps at headquarters confidently outlined the anticipated routes of advance to the Belgian border and beyond.

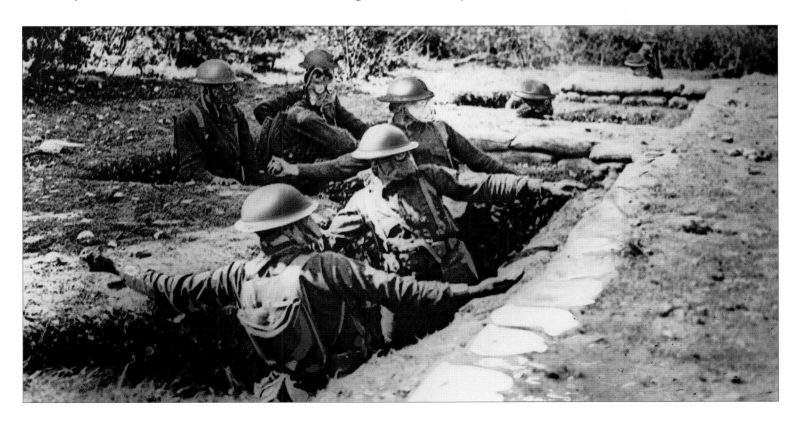

The Genesis of Stalemate

The reasons for the stalemate at the western front during the First World War are many and varied. First and foremost, the cost of crossing no-man's-land—the empty space separating the German and Allied lines—was extraordinarily high in the face of modern firepower. This meant an overwhelming superiority of men and munitions had to be brought to bear, and there were two problems related to the assembling of these masses: gathering great numbers of troops took a great deal of time, and more often than not the assembling of these troops signaled to the defender where the blow was going to fall. The advent of aerial reconnaissance made concealing one's offensive preparations especially difficult. Thus, few "big pushes" achieved any sort of surprise.

Even when the enemy's trench line had been broken, the attacker still faced many difficulties. In the days before wireless radios, messages to the rear had to be carried by runners until telephone lines could be run up to the leading units. And once field telephones were installed, their lines were cut by artillery fire with frustrating regularity. Coordination of reinforcements, resupply, and artillery fire therefore became almost impossible from the moment the men went over the top.

Logistically, large offensives were problematic, as they typically involved the coordination of several hundred thousand men on a front of about a dozen miles (19.2km). The defender also had some of these same problems, but its reserves operated on unscarred territory—while attackers had to slog across a muddy no-man's-land torn apart by weeklong barrages—and its communications were often dug 5 feet (1.5m) deep, rather than laid down onto the ground from a spool. As a result, it was almost always easier for the defender to rush reinforcements to a breach than it was for an attacker to push troops through one.

Finally, the sheer density of troops on the western front made any meaningful breakthrough virtually unattainable. In 1914 there were 2,000,000 German troops in the west. With a front that was about 400 miles (640km) long, this meant that there were roughly 5,000 German soldiers per mile (1.6km)—more than two men defending every yard (0.91m) of trench from the Channel to Switzerland.

Opposite: French poilus move along a communications trench that connects forward trenches with the rear. Below: Belgian soldiers line a canal near the town of Ypres, where one of the many battles of the Western Front occurred.

Right: Poilus prepare a trench mortar for action. Note the barbed wire and the flat, open terrain of no-man's-land.

Despite all this careful planning, however, a successful Anglo-French breakthrough was not to be. All this activity could not be hidden from the Germans, who had learned a few lessons themselves from the summer's conflicts. The Germans positioned reserves near the points of attack, just beyond the reach of Allied artillery. The front lines were thinned out and a second line constructed behind them. In this way, the fury of the opening bombardment would be spent on nearly empty trenches.

On September 25, the Allied offensive began. The opening barrage crashed down, followed closely by the assault waves, which easily overran the first line of resistance. Allied headquarters brimmed with optimism, but things quickly went awry. The violence of the bombardment had so greatly damaged the earth that troops had difficulty traversing the shell-pocked ground, and bringing up supporting artillery proved almost impossible. A shift in the wind blew their own gas (a choking agent, like chlorine or phosgene gas) back upon the British, disorganizing their advance and causing heavy casualties among the less well-trained units. Reserve troops were kept so close behind the first wave that German artillery soon broke up their formations, leaving commanders with no follow-up troops to push into and through gaps. Available reserves were too often thrown against surviving German strong points, rather than being used to exploit successes elsewhere. At root, though, the offensive's failure stemmed from the unexpected resistance of a well-organized German second line. Behind this line, the Germans could maneuver their reserves easily over untouched ground, while French and British formations labored across the moonlike landscape created by their own bombardment. By the end of the second day, it became clear that

the hoped-for breakthrough would never materialize, but the Allied generals displayed a stubborn willingness to sacrifice their men's lives for little gain, dragging the offensive into November. By November 8, when the Allies at last broke off their attacks, another 242,000 names had been added to the casualty lists, for an advance of perhaps 5 miles (8km).

The next major offensive on the western front was the first German effort to break the deadlock. The chief of the German General Staff, General Erich von Falkenhayn, had correctly surmised that a clean breakthrough was simply impossible (a conclusion it would take the ever-hopeful Allies another long year to reach). He instead opted for a battle of attrition. A German offensive toward Verdun, an ancient fortress city that epitomized the French will to resist, would certainly bring the bulk of the French army to the town's defense. Falkenhayn reasoned that by a series of carefully coordinated attacks, relying heavily on artillery support, he could bleed the French dry as they sent more and more forces to defend the city. The success or failure of the attacks in gaining ground was immaterial, as the sole object was to kill as many Frenchmen as possible—in fact, actually capturing Verdun would deprive the Germans of the bait with which they hoped to lure the French army to its death.

The attack opened on February 21, 1916. Crown Prince Rupprecht's Fifth Army eschewed the headlong rush that had decimated Allied attacks the previous year. Instead, violent bombardments preceded a cautious probing (a small-scale attack designed to find a weak spot in the enemy lines), after which the weakest points of the line were seized and consolidated. Any counterattacks by those Allied troops that were close at hand were beaten back, and the process repeated. All the while, French artillery positions and reserve formations were pounded mercilessly. In this way, the French positions were gradually eroded, and for once the defenders suffered greater losses than the attacker. One French regiment, for example, lost 1,800 of 2,000 men on the first day alone.

For several weeks the hellish battle continued, with casualties increasing at an astounding rate, while the German lines steadily approached Verdun. By early April, though, Falkenhayn sensed that the scales were beginning to tip to the French side. The French had indeed thrown every available division into the fight, and German daily casualties were beginning to approach those of the French. Pursuing the battle at this point, Falkenhayn believed, would be counterproductive—a strategy of attrition could only work if your opponent lost men at a greater rate than you. But the Germans now became victims of their own success. The prize of Verdun

The Allied solution to the stalemate: a tank leads the infantry across no-man's-land.

hung tantalizingly close, and Crown Prince Rupprecht demanded that the battle continue. Falkenhayn finally agreed, but then refused to supply sufficient men and ammunition to ensure the city's capture. As a result, in a long series of futile assaults that stretched through the month of July, German casualties soared but the city remained firmly in French hands. Eventually, the weakened Fifth Army was driven back almost to its starting lines by French counterattacks beginning in October.

The butcher's bill for Verdun stunned both armies. The French sacrificed 542,000 men to hold on to a city of little strategic value; though the French forces were not entirely decimated, they were rendered incapable of major offensive action for the foreseeable future. The Germans fared little better, losing 434,000 troops, the majority of them suffered after their ill-advised decision to continue the offensive past April.

Wonder Weapon II

In the spring of 1915, the Germans were about to launch an attack against the Anglo-French defenses around the Belgian town of Ypres. This action was less a true assault than it was an experiment designed to test the effectiveness of a new and insidious weapon: poison gas. German scientists had designed iron cylinders that released chlorine gas; all that was needed were suitable winds to propel the cloud toward Allied lines. At 5:00 P.M. on April 22, the spring breeze was blowing steadily westward toward Ypres.

Following a short covering bombardment, the chlorine was released. It worked magnificently. French, Algerian, and Canadian troops fled in abject terror, choking and vomiting, creating a 4-mile-wide (6.4km) gap without a single defender. German troops rushed forward, but the breach quickly closed. The Germans, who had not expected such a success, had not assembled reserves to exploit any openings created in the Anglo-French line. Moreover, the available troops were as ignorant of chemical warfare as the Allied soldiers. After a few miles' advance, the Germans ran into their own gas cloud and stopped, allowing British and Indian reserves, many of whom held urine-soaked handkerchiefs to their faces to counteract the lingering chlorine gas, to cobble together a line. Though they had gained a fair amount of land at little cost (by Great War standards), the Germans had squandered the surprise essential to the success of this new weapon; following the Battle of Ypres, French and British factories began turning out gas masks by the thousands.

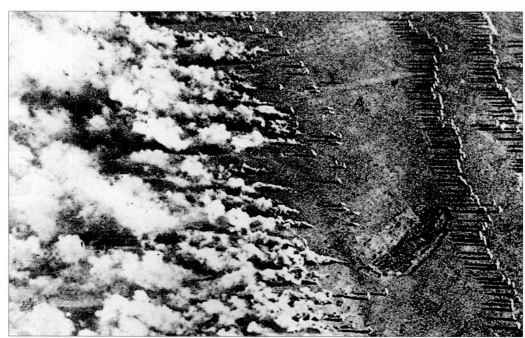

Above: The soldier at left pays the price for fumbling with his mask during a gas attack. Left: Allied troops train in the use of the gas mask. Right: Aerial view of a German gas attack. Clouds are released from cylinders to blow into Allied trenches. Gas could also be delivered using special artillery shells.

Above: British supply wagons haul forward more ammunition for another big push.

On the other end of the trench line, the Verdun battles influenced events along the banks of the Somme River. In order to relieve the pressure on the French, the British Army, now commanded by the mulish Haig, prepared an offensive slated for the end of June. An army of 500,000 men was assembled, along with tons of ammunition, engineering supplies, and wire, for an assault along the north bank. The main effort was to be made by the newly formed Fourth Army, led by General Sir Henry Rawlinson. The general planned to rely on an extremely heavy initial barrage, lasting for a solid week, to destroy the German lines, and then to have his infantry follow the exploding shells as the curtain of fire moved across the battlefield.

The barrage opened on June 24, and over the next seven days more than 1,600,000 shells rained down on the German lines. The Germans, however, had had two years to dig on this partic- ular stretch of front, and this time had been put to good use—even this tremendous bombardment did not completely wipe out the front trench line. Though dazed and deafened, enough Germans survived the artillery fire to man the defenses when the British went over the top on July 1.

Along a 15-mile (24km) front, 100,000 heavily laden British troops emerged from their trenches, trudging forward in neat lines toward enemy positions they believed to be empty save for the dead. Because most British officers believed that the biggest prob- lem would be keeping up with the creeping barrage, the men were kept well in hand, almost shoulder to shoul- der. Ahead of them the barrage at last shifted forward, allowing the Germans to scramble up from their dugouts. The sight that greeted them was one with which their great-grandfathers would have been familiar—infantry advancing steadily in dressed ranks, bent under bulging packs, bayonets fixed and glint- ing in the sun. Within moments, machine gun and rifle fire began to ruin the beautiful precision of the advancing waves. All along the dozen miles (19.2km) of the Somme battlefield, whole battalions were mowed down in an instant, the troops behind them stepping faithfully into the breach to be slaughtered in turn. Few troops even reached the German first line; those that did found the curtain of artillery fire had moved so far ahead (there was no way to signal the batteries that the infantry had been delayed) as to be use- less, meaning the second trench line was alert and ready for them. Here and there, small parties made their way to their objectives, only to be cut off and annihilated by German counterattacks.

Still, subsequent waves pressed the attack, until through sheer weight of numbers and incredible valor, a few of the attacking divisions were able to gain the first day's objectives (determined by estimating the rate of advance one could expect given the ratio of attackers to dug-in defenders). But Rawlinson, safely ensconced in his headquarters, did not support the successful sectors; instead, he threw his reserves in where resistance had been fiercest, so that he merely compounded the British failure. By the end of the day, by any measure, the Germans had stopped the British offensive in its tracks. Almost 60,000 British troops had been killed, captured, or wounded.

Incredibly, the offensive ground on until November with only intermittent breaks. At last, when the limits of human endurance and British manpower had been reached, the campaign sputtered to a close. Including French losses on the right flank of the offensive, the Allies lost 615,000 men, or roughly 100,000 for each mile (1.6km) the Germans were driven back. The Germans suffered a similar number of casualties, largely because of the imbecilic dictate of General Otto von Below, the local commander, that every inch of territory must be held to the last man and then retaken by immediate counterattack.

As 1916 drew to a close, all three major armies on the western front were reeling from exhaustion. Having tried massed infantry assaults, hurricane barrages, limited attacks, poison gas, and surprise attacks, and failed to break the enemy's line using any of these tactics, the commanders on each side allowed the front to lapse into relative somnolence while they regained their strength.

As stated before, the Allied commanders were not stupid men. By now, both Joffre and Haig had realized that the only road to victory lay through slow, grinding battles of attrition. There would be no breakthroughs to the green fields beyond the trench lines, no sudden eruption of cavalry to restore a war of mobility. Total war had doomed the western front to resemble the siege works before some medieval castle, and only the dirty, painful, tedious process of sapping the enemy's will while draining its manpower could bring the whole affair to an end.

But the wellspring of military ignorance had not yet run dry. Hard as it might be to credit, some commanders had resisted the hard lessons of the past two years. One such man was General Robert Nivelle, a Frenchman who somehow emerged from Verdun with the idea that, given the proper resources, he could split the German line in forty-eight hours. The French government much preferred his vision to Joffre's, and they sacked the venerable general in favor of Nivelle.

Nivelle immediately set about preparing for his grand offensive, assembling an impressive force that included 11 infantry corps, hundreds of heavy artillery pieces, and large numbers of tanks, which only recently had been introduced onto the battlefield. The fiery commander also somehow inspired his jaded soldiers with renewed enthusiasm for the attack and the promise of an early peace.

But Nivelle chose to execute his assault along a daunting stretch of the front. Attacking northward from the Aisne River, the French faced a series of steep, heavily wooded ridges, each strongly fortified by Germans now well versed in the tactical defensive. Furthermore, the operation was compromised by the capture of detailed plans, which Nivelle had unwisely circulated down to company level. Regardless of the breach in security, however, Nivelle refused to change his plans, even when he learned that trainloads of German troops were reinforcing the threatened sector.

On April 5, there began an eleven-day bombardment, which accomplished little besides confirming the location of the attack and churning the hillsides into a fine soup. On April 16, attacking French troops left their trenches behind a creeping barrage and struggled up onto the high ground. The attack quickly degenerated into a replay of all the disasters of 1915 and 1916. Trapped in the narrow confines between ridges, most of the tanks were destroyed by point-blank artillery fire; massed machine gun fire and counter-barrages tore the attacking formations to shreds, while local counterattacks mopped up the survivors. Despite bleak prospects of success, Nivelle bullheadedly fed reserves into the meat grinder, sacrificing division after division in the vain hope that one more push might do the trick. Within three days, even the politicians had had enough; Nivelle was recalled to Paris to explain the reasons for this new debacle, though most front-line soldiers could have explained it easily enough.

This latest defeat nearly broke the French Army. Within the next few weeks, 54 divisions mutinied, most promising to remain on the defensive, but otherwise refusing to leave their trenches. Nivelle had at last exhausted the endurance of the poilus—a remarkable achievement considering what they had put up with in the past. Luckily for the Allies, the Germans obtained no inkling of the uprising, and the mutinies were put down before permanent damage was done.

It would be wearisome and repetitive to discuss in detail the remaining year of stalemate on the western front, before the arrival of fresh American troops and the utter exhaustion of the German Army brought an end to the war. Suffice it to say that in 1918 the opposing armies at last found diverse ways to penetrate the trench lines and restore some measure of mobility to the battlefield. For the Allies, the tank, employed in large numbers on suitable terrain, provided a way to overcome the strength of the machine gun. The Germans, for their part, developed infiltration tactics whereby strong points were bypassed by small groups of specially trained stormtroopers sent in to sow confusion in the rear areas while reserves mopped up isolated holdouts on the front line. But ultimately it was the arrival of American reinforcements and the state of the demoralized German army, not any brilliance on the part of any particular general, that finally ended the fighting.

Conclusion

In the early morning hours of February 24, 1991, a group of helicopters bearing soldiers of the U.S. 101st Airborne Division (Air Assault) lifted off from their desert bases in Saudi Arabia. They headed north into Iraq, followed by the tanks and mechanized columns of XVIII Airborne Corps. By midmorning, the greatest armored force ever assembled was churning virtually unopposed through the sandy wastes of southern Iraq. In less than two days, this force reached the Euphrates River, effectively cutting off the greater part of the fourth largest army in the world. Thirty-six hours after that, Iraq's vaunted Republican Guard was defeated, and its armaments lay shattered and smoking amidst the wreckage of the Kuwaiti oil fields.

The Republican Guard perished partly because the Allied forces possessed command of the air and a decided technological advantage; however, the blunders of the erstwhile Iraqi dictator, Saddam Hussein, also contributed heavily to their defeat. Hussein not only had badly underestimated "the reaction and resolve of the American people and their allies, but also had misjudged the capabilities of the American army. Believing that no modern mechanized force could traverse the trackless Saudi Arabian desert west of his lines, he had left his right flank hanging in the air. It was this open flank that XVIII Airborne Corps took advantage of, bypassing the heavily fortified sectors along the Kuwaiti–Saudi Arabian border. Once into the Iraqi rear, the Allied armored forces smashed the divisions of the Republican Guard one by one. Within a hundred hours of the start of the ground campaign, Hussein asked for an armistice.

Saddam Hussein is living proof that, even in age of smart bombs, satellite reconnaissance, laser-guided munitions, and surface-to-surface missiles, the military blunderer survives; indeed, it is likely that Saddam's blunders will be studied in military colleges well into the next century, if not the next several hundred years. In fact, looking back over the nearly eight decades since the First World War, one can see that the opportunities and scope for fools in uniform have only increased.

The roll call of disasters has lengthened considerably since 1918: Sedan, Dunkirk, Crete, Pearl Harbor, Dieppe, Stalingrad, the Bulge, Chosin Reservoir, Dien Bien Phu, the Sinai, Khe Sanh, Yom Kippur, and the Falklands, which will be covered in the sequel to this book, are only a few of the better-known examples. The cast of characters has also expanded: chateaux-bound French generals sitting helplessly at their desks as the panzers roll by; Adolf Hitler pushing colored flags around his maps while the Third Reich crumbles; Douglas MacArthur, who balanced a brilliant career with some of the century's worst military errors; American generals armed with flow charts and computer printouts losing to sandal-clad guerillas in Vietnam; Arab commanders unable to withstand the onslaught of an outgunned, outnumbered Israeli army.

In a world in which technological and social changes are continually accelerating, chances are that it will become more and more difficult for soldiers to adjust to changing circumstances. The speed and violence of present-day warfare are rapidly approaching the limits of human endurance, but the humming computers and advanced communications that make it possible to fight in this milieu have not eliminated the darker side of human nature. Hubris, fear, miscalculation, and incompetence still exist beside the gleaming weaponry of the twentieth century, making future blunders almost inevitable.

The best that can be said is that mankind has so far avoided the ultimate military blunder. No commander-in-chief has been mad enough, or desperate enough, to unleash the nuclear-tipped missiles that still wait patiently below ground or nestled in the bowels of submarines.

Top: War takes a great toll, not only on those who fight in it, but on the fields and villages where it is fought. This sinister image shows the incredible destruction wrought by the near-endless fighting in western Europe during the First World War. Above: Hell breaks loose in Flanders: In this moment of chaos on the western front, a British tank bursts into flames over a fallen soldier while in the background a tank crashes through a line of barbed wire, follwed by a group of British infantrymen.

Bibliography

Bond, Brian, ed. *Victorian Military Campaigns.* New York: Frederick A. Praeger, Publishers, 1967.

Brent, Peter. *Ghenghis Khan.* New York: McGraw-Hill Book Company, 1976.

Brett-James, Antony. *1812: Eyewitness Accounts of Napoleon's Defeat in Russia.* New York: St. Martin's Press, 1966.

Brooks, Charles B. *The Siege of New Orleans.* Seattle: University of Washington Press, 1961.

Buist, Francis, and Katherine Tomasson. *Battles of the '45.* New York: The MacMillan Company, 1962.

Burne, Alfred H. *The Crecy War.* New York: Oxford University Press, 1955.

Cate, Curtis. "Rocroi," *Military History Quarterly.* Vol. II, No. 1 (Autumn 1989), pp. 24–31.

Catton, Bruce. *Never Call Retreat.* Garden City, N.Y.: Doubleday & Company, Inc., 1965.

Chambers, James. *The Devil's Horsemen.* New York: Atheneum, 1979.

Chandler, David. *Battlefields of Europe* (2 vols.). New York: Chilton Books, 1965.

_____. *The Campaigns of Napoleon.* New York: The MacMillan Company, 1966.

Cocceianus, Cassius Dio. *Dio's Roman History* (4 vols.). Trans. Herbert Baldwin Foster. Troy, N.Y.: Pafraets Book Company, 1905.

Crackel, Theodore J. *The Illustrated History of West Point.* New York: Harry N. Abrams, Inc., 1991.

Delderfield, Ronald. *Napoleon's Marshals.* New York: Chilton Books, 1966.

_____. *The Retreat From Moscow.* New York: Atheneum, 1967.

Duffy, Christopher. *Austerlitz 1805.* Hamden, Conn.: Archon Books, 1977.

_____. *Borodino and the War of 1812.* New York: Charles Scribner's Sons, 1973.

Esposito, Vincent J., ed. *The West Point Atlas of American Wars* (2 vols.). New York: Praeger Publishers, 1972.

Fair, Charles. *From the Jaws of Victory.* New York: Simon and Schuster, 1971.

Falls, Cyril. *The Great War.* New York: G.P. Putnam's Sons, 1959.

Farwell, Byron. *Queen Victoria's Little Wars.* New York: Harper & Row, Publishers, 1972.

Foote, Shelby. *The Civil War: A Narrative.* New York: Random House, 1963.

Freeman, Douglas Southall. *Lee's Lieutenants: A Study in Command.* New York: Charles Scribner's Sons, 1944.

Fuller, J.F.C. *Decisive Battles: Their Influence Upon History and Civilization.* New York: Charles Scribner's Sons, 1940.

Grousset, Rene. *Conqueror of the World.* Trans. Marian McKellar and Denis Sinor. New York: The Orion Press, 1966.

Hamilton, Charles, ed. *Braddock's Defeat.* Normal, Okla.: University of Oklahoma Press, 1959.

Hart, B.H. Liddel. *The Real War 1914–1918.* Boston: Little, Brown and Company, 1930.

Howard, Michael. *The Franco-Prussian War.* London: Routledge, 1988.

Johnson, Swafford. *History of the U.S. Cavalry.* Greenwich, Conn.: Bison Books Corp., 1985.

Judd, Denis. *The Crimean War.* London: Hart-Davis, MacGibbon Ltd., 1975.

_____. *Someone Has Blundered.* London: Arthur Barker Limited, 1973.

Karl, Dennis. *Glorious Defiance.* New York: Paragon House, 1990.

King, Sir Lucas. *Memoirs of Zehir-ed-Din Muhammed Babur*. Trans. John Leyden and William Erskine. London: Oxford University Press, 1921.

Knecht, R.J. *Francis I*. Cambridge: Cambridge University Press, 1982.

Kwanten, Luc. *Imperial Nomads: A History of Central Asia 500–1500*. Philadelphia: University of Pennsylvania Press, 1979.

Luvaas, Jay, and Harold W. Nelson, eds. *The U.S. Army War College Guide to the Battles of Chancellorsville and Fredericksburg*. New York: Harper & Row, Publishers, 1988.

Marcus, Harold. *The Life and Times of Menelik II*. Oxford: Clarendon Press, 1975.

Marshall, Robert. *Storm From the East: From Ghenghis Khan to Khubilai Khan*. Los Angeles: University of California Press, 1993.

Maurice, J.F., ed. and trans. *The Franco-German War 1870–71*. London: Swan, Sonnenschein and Co.

McEntee, Girard. *Military History of the World War*. New York: Charles Scribner's Sons, 1943.

Morgan, David. *The Mongols*. Cambridge, Mass.: Basil Blackwell, Inc., 1986.

Morris, Donald R. *The Washing of the Spears*. New York: Simon and Schuster, 1965.

Pakenham, Thomas. *The Scramble for Africa, 1876–1912*. New York: Random House, 1991.

Parker, Geoffrey. *The Thirty Years War*. New York: Military Heritage Press, 1984.

Peckham, Howard. *The Colonial Wars 1689–1762*. Chicago: University of Chicago Press, 1964.

Pemberton, William B. *Battles of the Boer War*. London: B.T. Batsford, Ltd., 1964.

_____. *Battles of the Crimean War*. New York: The MacMillan Company, 1962.

Perroy, Edouard. *The Hundred Years War*. Trans. W.B. Wells. Bloomington, Ind.: Indiana University Press, 1959.

Ratchnevsky, Paul. *Ghenghis Khan: His Life and Legacy*. Trans. and ed. Thomas N. Haining. Cambridge, Mass.: Blackwell Publishers, 1991.

Selby, John. *The Road to Yorktown*. New York: St. Martin's Press, 1976.

Scullard, Howard H. *The Elephant in the Greek and Roman World*. Ithaca, N.Y.: Cornell University Press, 1974.

Seward, Desmond. *Prince of the Rennaissance*. New York: MacMillan Publishing Co., Inc., 1973.

Simkins, Michael. *The Roman Army from Caesar to Trajan*. New York: Hippocrene Books, Inc., 1973.

Sixsmith, Eric K.S. *British Generalship in the Twentieth Century*. London: Arms and Armour Press, 1970.

Srivastava, Ashirbadilal. *The History of India 1000 A.D –1707 A.D*. Agra, India: Shiva Lal Agarwala & Co., Ltd., 1964.

Stagg, J.C.A. *Mr. Madison's War*. Princeton, N.J.: Princeton University Press, 1983.

Tacitus. *Complete Works of Tacitus*. Ed. Moses Hadas. New York: Random House, Inc., 1942.

Warry, John. *Warfare in the Classical World*. London: Salamander Books, Ltd., 1980.

Wedgewood, C.V. *The Thirty Years War*. Garden City, N.Y.: Doubleday & Company, Inc., 1961.

Weigley, Russell. *The Age of Battles*. Indianapolis, Ind.: Indiana University Press, 1991.

Williams, L.F. Rushbrook. *An Empire Builder of the Sixteenth Century*. London: Longmans, Green, and Co., 1913.

Williams, T. Harry. *Lincoln and His Generals*. New York: Vintage Books, 1952.

Wise, Terence. *Medieval Warfare*. New York: Hastings House Publishers, Inc., 1976.

Woodham-Smith, Cecil. *The Reason Why*. New York: G.P. Dutton & Co., Inc., 1960.

Index

Photography Credits

© Anne S. K. Brown Military Collection, Brown University Library: pp. 87 top, 88–89, 90

AP/Wide World Photos: pp. 2 inset, 74 bottom

Archive Photos: pp. 3, 6, 7, 16, 26 top right, 28 top right, 31 right, 37 left, 48, 51, 52 top, 53 right, 87 bottom, 91, 97, 104; © Hirz: pp. 5, 92

© Archiv fur Kunst und Geschichte, Berlin: pp. 13, 14, 95 left, 96

Art Resource, N.Y.: © **Giraudon**: pp. 9, 10, 34 top, 42 top, 50, 53 left, 54, 58 bottom, 60; © **Lauros-Giraudon**: pp. 40–41; © **Erich Lessing**: pp. 21, 33 top, 34 bottom; © **National Portrait Gallery/Smithsonian Institution**: p. 56 inset; © **Scala**: pp. 24 top, 35, 94 top; © **SEF**: p. 100; © **The Board of Trustees of the Victoria & Albert Museum**: p. 37 right

Bettmann Archive: pp. 11, 17 bottom, 22, 26 top left, bottom left, and bottom right, 28 top left, 33 bottom, 45 top left, 46, 47 top, 65 top, 66 top, 73, 82 bottom, 85 left, 86 top, 103 bottom, 107, 108 both, 109 bottom, 110, 112, 113 both

© The British Library: *Babur's Battle Against the Rana of Mewar*, p. 38

© FPG International: pp. 78, 93, 103 top, 106

© Hulton Deutsch Collection: pp. 39 top, 42 bottom, 43, 45 top right and bottom, 81, 82 inset, 83 top, 84, 85 right, 95 right, 105

© Kurz & Allison Art Publishers/Superstock: pp. 2 bottom, 77 top

Library of Congress: pp. 64 top, 65 bottom, 67 bottom, 69, 71

© Montana Historical Society, Gift of the Artist: *Last Stop on Battle Ridge*, Gary Zaboly: p. 75

© National Army Museum, London: Charles Fripp, *The Last Stand at Isandhula* [Isandhlwana]: p. 80

North Wind Picture Archives: pp. 15, 18, 19, 24 bottom, 28 bottom, 49, 56, 57 bottom, 58 top, 66 bottom, 76, 98 bottom

© 17th/21st Lancers' Museum, Belvoir Castle: *The Charge of the 21st Lancers at Omdurman*, by Geroge Delville Rowlandson: p. 72

Stock Montage, Inc: pp. 23, 25 bottom, 27, 30, 31 left, 62–63, 67 top, 70, 79 right, 83 bottom, 99

Western History Collection, University of Oklahoma Library: p. 77 bottom

All map illustrations by Steven Stankiewicz